Growth of
the Modern
American Economy

May 15, 1975

*For Bob,
with affection.
Stu*

IRWIN UNGER
New York University
Consulting Editor

Growth of the Modern American Economy

Stuart Bruchey

Allan Nevins Professor
American Economic History
COLUMBIA UNIVERSITY

DODD, MEAD & COMPANY
New York   1975

For Andy and Sammy

No part of this book may be reproduced in any
form without permission in writing from the publisher

Library of Congress Catalog Card Number: 74-26155

ISBN: 0-396-07091-4

Printed in the United States of America

Designed by Jeffrey M. Barrie

Editor's Introduction

Economic development is one of the great problems of the modern world. Everywhere—in Latin America, Africa, and Southeast Asia—both new and old nations are struggling to find ways to raise the living levels of their people. Even in the oil-rich Arab lands and in the developed countries of Western Europe and North America, the issues of economic growth are still very much alive. Although most of the developed countries have actually achieved a high-level income for their citizens on the average, they (and this includes the United States) are anxious for continued improvement and are concerned with how growth may be made compatible with an attractive and humane environment for all their people. How the very richest and most economically powerful nation of the developed West managed in the space of less than two hundred years to move from an overwhelmingly agricultural base to an industrial one, and how it managed to raise the living level of its citizens to the highest in the world, are the themes of this book.

In the past two decades, the discipline of economic history has been transformed. The challenging and unsettling struggles of the Third World for economic growth have directed the attention of economists toward the past experiences of modern developed nations. Advances in economic theory, as well as progress in applying statistical techniques made possible by electronic computers, have given economists new tools of investigation and analysis. Joined together, these new concerns and approaches have created a "new economic history" that has attracted much attention.

The insights of this new economic history have added immeasurably to our understanding of how economic development takes place in the present, and have also told us much of how it took place in the past. Moreover, concerns about both past and present have marvelously cross-fertilized one another so that today we know far more than we ever did about the way poor nations have become rich, or at least richer. Stuart Bruchey is not primarily a "cliometrician," as the new breed of computer-oriented historians are called. His formal training has been as an historian. Yet, while retaining the traditional historian's understanding of institutions and human motives, he has sought to master and to present the findings and insights of these scholars.

As a case study of the process of economic development, the economic history of the United States in the nineteenth and twentieth centuries is particularly interesting. Not because it was typical. It was not. Even at the beginning of the nineteenth century, the United States had one of the highest per capita Gross National Products in the world—the result of an outstanding "mix" of abundant resources and a talented, enterprising, and well-educated labor force. Few other countries could boast the high proportion to population of fertile land, excellent timber, iron ore, coal and water power that the

United States possessed. The use that the country made of its advantages and the way it overcame its inevitable handicaps must be of interest not only to students of American history but also to those concerned with the general problems of economic growth. In compact form Professor Bruchey gives us the best of the new research in American economic history plus the contribution of his own insights into the course taken by the "first new nation."

IRWIN UNGER

Preface

I have written this book in an effort to distill many of the recent findings of American economic historians into language that can be understood by all. The book is nontechnical in nature and intended for undergraduates in history and economics. Nevertheless, I hope that graduate students in these and other social sciences, and a general reading audience that is increasingly debating the benefits and costs of economic growth, will also find it of interest. It is of course a very brief book, one that is synoptic rather than detailed.

Economic growth is usually defined as a sustained increase in real output percapita—an increase that results from rising inputs of the productive factors of land, labor, and capital, and of growth in the efficiency with which they are used. In this book I concentrate on the main sources of efficiency and on changes in those sources over time. As an historian, I have followed a chronological presentation, and in selecting time periods to frame the discussion I have been guided by the interests of recent scholarship.

One such interest is the question whether economic growth occurred in the period before roughly 1840, and this accounts for the time period covered by Chapter 1, "The Agricultural Republic, 1790–1840," so titled to accentuate the dominant form of production in those years. Another interest lies in the nature and pace of change in the final two decades of the antebellum period—especially in whether or not a "takeoff" into self-sustained growth occurred during that period—and the title of Chapter 2, "The Challenge of Industry, 1840–60," reflects a judgment on the character of the leading edge of growth in these years.

Chapter 3, "The Civil War and the Postwar Industrial Revolution, 1861–1914," opens with a brief review of the recent debate on the economic impact of the Civil War. After the evidence relevant to this issue has been presented, several pages are devoted to a discussion of the nature of the process by which defensible historical generalizations are made. Even a brief methodological foray, I realize, generally belongs in a preface or epilogue, but I have put this one where it is in the hope that the point can more clearly be seen in relation to a specific historical application. The great bulk of Chapter 3 is devoted to developments in the period 1865–1914. My view that the term "American Industrial Revolution" is more suitably applied to this period than to any earlier one represents a departure from emphases currently in favor. I can therefore only hope that the reasons assigned for my return to a more traditional point of view will be found of interest to my readers.

The final chapter, "The Technological Thrust of the Twentieth Century," like its predecessors, focuses on underlying sources of productivity change rather than upon the impact of war and governmental policies. It is unquestionably true that the role of government in the economy of the twentieth century has been one of increasing importance, particularly in the areas of monetary and fiscal policy since World War II. It is no less true that the twentieth century has witnessed the comparative decline of commodity production and the rise of a "service economy," and that the latter makes for added difficulties in the assessment of the growth of output and productivity. Labor relations have been transformed by the emergence and growth of national unions and industrial unions, by the rise of industrywide collective bargaining, and by stabilization of the size of the unionized sector of the labor force. The United States itself has emerged as a major political as well as industrial power; it is the legatee of the nineteenth-century imperialist nations, the successor of Britain in its hegemony in the world of international finance.

But I do not discuss these things. These and other developments are undoubtedly pertinent to any analysis of short-run alterations in the trend rates of growth. But no selective treatment of two centuries of economic change can hope to achieve balance between the long and short of things, and I have intentionally not written the kind of book which tries. What has been lacking, it has seemed to me, is a discussion of changes in the major sources of our growth in the various time periods into which one may usefully divide the last two centuries. I have tried to supply that lack, not by full and rounded analysis of all sources of growth in each of the periods, but rather by a selective emphasis featuring the process of change.

One final matter should be addressed in this introductory note. Why write a book on economic growth at all? Were not the 1950s and early 1960s the era of worldwide interest in growth? Is not the mood of the 1970s instead one of critical disillusionment with growth's products: environmental pollution, resource depletion, congestion, litter, noise, insecurity, and a host of other ills? Is not growth obsolete?

Many—but not all—of these accusations are well-founded. In the final chapter I address myself explicitly to them and to other recently discussed subjects, including the impact of growth on poverty. Yet even if the nation were to turn its back upon the goal of growth, even if it were to heed Paul Ehrlich's warning that "We must acquire a life style which has as its goal maximum freedom and happiness for the individual, not a maximum Gross National Product," it does not follow that we should reject the theme of growth in interpreting our history. To do so, I believe, would gravely distort a central objective of generations of Americans.

But my own view goes beyond this. I believe it would be premature to abandon the goal of growth. Economic growth has done more than the general public realizes to reduce poverty in this country, and its historically growing need for improvement in the quality of human capital must be reckoned among the vital factors making for a truer social democracy. As for degradation of the environment, it is policy, not growth, that is at fault: the adoption of public policies designed to remove the incentives business firms now have for fouling the air and polluting the waters would go far to arrest these reprehensible practices. This matter, too, is discussed in the final chapter.

ACKNOWLEDGMENTS

Since this is a book that summarizes and interprets the work of many scholars, its obligations to others will be apparent to even the casual reader. Yet there are a few who gave more than this. If my book turns out to be a useful one, much of the credit will be due to the generosity of the following persons.

Alfred D. Chandler, Jr., shared with me his deep knowledge of the ways in which the American economy changed and saved me from a number of factual errors. So did my colleague Peter Passell, who had the opportunity to read the opening chapter before embarking last year on a distant leave of absence. Stanley L. Engerman is rapidly becoming known as the critical conscience of our profession. This acknowledgment of his never-failing help and advice, gently but incisively given to so many of us, is but one among dozens to be found in the pages of the *Journal of Economic History* and elsewhere. I find it difficult to express adequately my indebtedness to Paul A. David. When I read his critique I wondered how often it is that a manuscript receives such a searching review. Correcting errors of fact and pointing to theoretical implications of which I had been unaware, Paul David gave me the benefit of what I am persuaded is one of the finest critical minds of our time.

I want also to express my appreciation to Irwin Unger, the general editor of the series in which this volume appears, to Charles Woodford, Senior Editor, and Genia Graves, Managing Editor of the College Department at Dodd, Mead and Company. All three have improved the book by their suggestions for change. Irwin Unger's sense of style caught many a stumbling phrase before it fell upon the printed page. In addition, his knowledge of American economic history saved me from a number of mistakes. My thanks go also to Stanley Lebergott, who never failed of a generous response to any of my questions—even when awakened early on a Sunday morning!—during our year together as members of the Institute for Advanced Study in Princeton. My thanks, too, to Joseph Paranac for his help on the index. Finally, I want to express to Dr. James McCampbell, University Librarian at the University of Maine in Orono, and to his staff, my appreciation for numerous and extended courtesies over the years.

To all these friends: thanks. The inadequacies that remain are my own.

STUART BRUCHEY

Contents

Tables

ONE

The Agricultural Republic, 1790–1840

In twentieth-century America a principal determinant of economic growth is the quality of the nation's stock of human resources. The latter, in turn, largely depends upon the quality of education and, quite possibly, upon the degree to which education permeates the population. Human capital is as important as it has been in recent growth because of the vital role played by organized knowledge in production. Technological advances made possible by that knowledge have gone far in the twentieth century to replace scarce natural resources with a vast range of synthetic materials whose ingredients have no counterpart in nature. The extent to which this will continue to be the case, especially the extent to which the search for substitutes for depletable sources of energy will prove successful, together probably pose the most important economic questions before the United States in the later years of the twentieth century. Even these considerations, however—vital as they are—cannot alter the historical record, cannot change what has already been accomplished by the advance of knowledge in this century. Thus far its role has been a preeminent one.

It was not always so. In earlier times our abundance of natural resources in relation to the population acted as a prime engine of growth. Because geologic and climatic differences between the principal geographic regions of the country strongly influenced the distribution of resources and because the nation's rate of growth reflected differences in the economic performance of its regions, we begin our account with a brief description of these variations in the resource base of the new nation.

In 1790 the American people numbered just under four million persons, of whom 3,172,000 were white and 757,000 nonwhite. Most of the nonwhites were blacks, and either they themselves or their ancestors had been brought as slaves from Africa. The majority of the whites were English in origin, although Scotland, Ireland, Germany, Holland, and other countries of northwestern Europe also contributed to the makeup of the population. For the most part, the population of 1790 was composed not of immigrants but of persons who had been born in America. It was a youthful population, for the median age of white males was 15.9 years. And in all probability it was a healthy and literate population. The former is suggested not only by a number of local studies of colonial America but also by the fact that outbreaks of virulent disease—for example, of yellow fever in Philadelphia in 1793 and in

Baltimore in 1800—appear to have been confined to urban locales. Since in 1790 only 5 percent of the population lived in urban places (2,500 or more people), relatively few people would have been affected by such outbreaks. As for literacy, we have the recent judgment of Albert Fishlow that "it is probable that education was being prosecuted with comparable vigor over the whole period" from the beginning of the nineteenth century to 1840. This generalization, of course, excludes blacks, who as slaves were kept in ignorance as well as physical bondage.

The area occupied by the population in 1790 consisted in the main of a tier of Atlantic states stretching from Maine through Georgia. Movement to the west had begun to gather speed since the Revolution, however, and by 1790 Kentucky and the Southwest Territory boasted a population in excess of 100,000, of whom 15,000 were slaves. While a few slaves were to be found in New England and more in the Middle Atlantic states, the great majority—633,000 of the total 697,000—inhabited the South Atlantic states from Maryland to Georgia. Slaves dominated the 1790 census of nonwhites, for of the total 757,000, merely 60,000 were classified as free. The economic consequences of slavery for the antebellum South, and for the nation in the long run, are important questions that we shall consider in later chapters.

Meanwhile we should note that the paucity of slaves in New England was not owing to the Puritan origins of many of the inhabitants—in the colonial period Puritans had both owned slaves and participated in the slave trade—but principally, in all probability, to features of the region's physical environment. The dimensions of New England's arable land made it an area of limited agricultural possibilities, for the coastal plain that stretches between tidewater and mountains is only from fifty to eighty miles wide. In contrast, in the Carolinas the mountains are 250 miles from the sea. Furthermore, most of the surface of the region rests on rocks that are geologically old and very hard. Thousands of years ago the continental ice sheet wrenched off boulders and stones from the mountains across which it moved and strewed them over the lower lands. Glaciation made some parts of the region so rocky that they could not be plowed. In others, only coarse sand was left. In still others, though, as in the Connecticut Valley, the fertile alluvial soil equaled that of any agricultural area in the country.

New England was also handicapped by its climate. Winters were long and cold and a deep mantle of snow might cover the ground for three, four, or even five months. For the most part slaves would have been idle during these months, but still requiring to be fed, clothed and sheltered. In the South they could be employed during the mild winters in mending fences, digging weeds, cutting down trees, and in other occupations essential to the maintenance of staple agriculture. In addition, the longer growing season allowed them to be used for a much larger part of the year as husbandmen, their primary occupation. Furthermore, the cost of clothing and shelter in the colder North would have placed northerners at a competitive disadvantage in bidding for slaves. Southerners, that is to say, could have afforded to offer higher purchase prices because of lower maintenance costs in their region.

While New England had fewer arable acres than more southerly regions in possession of a wider coastal plain, those acres were far from lacking in fertility. Indeed, according to a contemporary, Samuel Blodget, in the early 1790s at least, average yields per acre of wheat, rye, barley, oats, Indian corn, and potatoes exceeded yields in New York, Pennsylvania, New Jersey, Delaware, Virginia, and the Carolinas. Some of these crops were produced in sufficient quantities for the coasting and export trades, as were lumber, livestock, and flax. Nevertheless, the total amounts were small in comparison with those of more favored agricultural areas. We may summarize by observing that New England was a region of small farms tilled by the labor of fathers and sons and, probably to a greater degree than elsewhere east of the mountains, tilled for purposes of family consumption. Clearly, the region's comparative advantages lay elsewhere than in agriculture.

Once again, nature played an important part in determining these advantages. Possessed of a sunken coast full of bays, as well as rivers with wide estuaries and forests rich in pine, New Englanders had turned early in their history to shipbuilding and trade. And because the more important food fish are more plentiful in cold water than in warm, the shores of the region and its outlying fishing banks proved hospitable to that industry. An abundance of water power was a major reason for New England's early eminence in textile manufacturing. The prehistoric glacier had sent the rivers into strange courses and provided hundreds of small waterfalls. These falls were unusually dependable, in part because the rainfall of the region is well distributed throughout the year. The glacier had also left upland swamps and thousands of lakes. Moreover, it had made many of the soils porous and thus able to absorb much rain, store it, and release it gradually through springs. A plentiful supply, in combination with evenness of flow, meant that, in contrast with regions below the glacial belt, dams were less likely to be washed out or raceways broken.

The soil and climate of the middle states made that region generally more hospitable to agriculture than was the case in New England. While the sandy soil of New Jersey's coastal plain had discouraged even the settlement of that area, the clay soils of the Piedmont, which ran through the northwestern part of New Jersey and on into Pennsylvania, were generally fertile. So too were the central valleys of New York and Pennsylvania, where layers of limestone had decomposed to form unusually rich agricultural land. On the whole, the land between the Potomac and the Hudson was the best in the new nation for the production of food, especially the cereal crops. Wheat was the most important crop, although the region also produced considerable quantities of corn, rye, oats, and barley, as well as livestock. As in New England, farms were operated by the farmer and his family, including, in the case of the Pennsylvania Germans, the help of women in the fields.

The great export staples were produced in the states from Maryland to Georgia. During the colonial period these had included tobacco, indigo, and rice, the production and export of which had been encouraged not only by British legislation but also by the fact that the soil and climate of the region gave a comparative advantage to crops in great demand in the industrial areas of the world. Tobacco required fertile soil, a long growing season, and meticulous care. A great deal of hand labor was needed to hoe the plant, remove worms, pick off buds to prevent blooming, break off young shoots so that only a single stalk remained, and finally to strip the leaves from the stalk and prepare them for market. Slaves—women and children, as well as men—performed this labor in the tobacco fields of Maryland and Virginia, and elsewhere in the South where smaller portions of the crop were grown. Much labor was needed too in the growing of rice, the culture of which finally extended from below Savannah up into North Carolina. Using a "task" system, planters assigned each slave a particular piece of ground to cultivate. The work was back-breaking, and it was carried on in hot, mosquito-infested swamps, characteristics that led to a high mortality rate among the men engaged in it. However, not only in 1790 but also throughout the antebellum period the South was far more than a land of staple agriculture and slavery. Both on plantations worked by slave gangs and on small farms worked by family labor the region produced large quantities of corn and hay, livestock and animal products, and a wide variety of fruits and vegetables.

While the census returns for 1790 show that 95 percent of the population was rural, it would be a mistake to believe that the activities of rural people were confined to agriculture. Specialization in agriculture as in other pursuits is dependent upon the existence of a substantial demand, and also upon an organization of economic activity that is sufficiently well developed to permit an easy exchange of goods and services. Most domestic markets were merely local, with exchanges of goods between regions mainly being confined to places accessible to seaborne commerce. Not only did difficulties of transport and communication limit the size of markets, free exchanges were also inhibited by an inadequate supply of money or of acceptable credit instruments; this encouraged barter, especially in backcountry transactions. For all these reasons, and also because of the seasonal nature of agricultural activity, inhabitants of rural regions produced a wide range of nonagricultural goods—and provided such services as blacksmithing and transport as well—for sale on local markets and for consumption by the households producing them. According to the historian of manufactures in the United States, Victor S. Clark, even in the early years of the nineteenth century "the self-subsisting farm household remained the typical economic unit of rural America; and homespun industries still supplied a large part of the nation's consumption."

Because of imperfect communications between small clusters of population living over an extended area, these clusters were necessarily largely self-subsisting, so that the spinning and weaving of cloth in the home, as well as such neighborhood manufactures as sawmilling, the reduction of iron from ores in bloomeries, and handicraft trades were widely dispersed rather than geographically concentrated. That some concentration existed in or near large urban areas, however, is evident from the following list of manufactures cited by Tench Coxe as being produced in the vicinity of Philadelphia in 1787:

> meal of all kinds, ships and boats, malt liquors, distilled spirits, potash, gunpowder, cordage, loaf-sugar, pasteboard, cards and paper of every kind, books in various languages, snuff, tobacco, starch, cannon, musquets, anchors, nails and very many other articles of iron, bricks, tiles, potter's ware, millstones and other stonework, cabinet work, trunks and windsor chairs, carriages and harness of all kinds, cornfans, ploughs, and many other implements of husbandry, saddlery and ships, shoes and boots, leather of various kinds, hosiery, hats and gloves, wearing apparel, coarse linens and woolens, and some cotton goods, linseed and fish oil, wares of gold, silver, tin, pewter, lead, brass and copper, clocks and watches, wool and cotton cards, printing type, glass and stone ware, candles, soap, and several other valuable articles, with which the memory cannot furnish us at once.

The list is long and impressive, but we do not know what quantities were produced either here or elsewhere in the nation—and hence we are ignorant of the aggregate value of manufacturing output. It cannot have been large. In 1810, only about 3 percent of the nation's total labor force was employed in factory production. To be sure, the percentage engaged in manufacturing would be considerably larger than that if we knew how many smiths, cobblers, and other artisans were practicing their crafts. We do have estimates of the value of manufactures produced in rural homes, but these are assigned to the agricultural rather than to the manufacturing sector. Despite these uncertainties, the assumption that agricultural output far exceeded manufacturing output in value is warranted. This is true not only for 1800, when 82.6 percent of the labor force was engaged in agriculture, but also for 1840, when 63.4 percent was so engaged.

While we can be sure of the predominance of agriculture before 1840—and for many years thereafter as well—it is much more difficult to speak with confidence about the changing value of agricultural output. The reason for this is that federal censuses before 1840 have little to say about agriculture, or about manufacturing either, for that matter. Indeed, early censuses are so poor in these respects as to have been called "almost worthless" by one scholar. In consequence, historians at work in this statistical half-light have had to make what use they could of surviving fragmentary materials, to extrapolate backwards from later periods, and to indulge in bold assumptions. But while they are confident that such procedures are to be preferred to the rhetoric of uncontrolled conjecture, they are quick to emphasize, as Robert E. Gallman has, "the deficiencies in the available evidence and to advise the reader to use the results derived . . . with great caution."

With these words of warning Gallman introduces the tentative results of his effort to assemble and refine measures of the gross value of agricultural output between 1800 and 1840. Conceiving output broadly to include not only crops and livestock, but also home manufactures and firewood, he estimates growth to have taken place during this interval at an average annual rate of 3.11 percent.

What made this growth possible was an increase in the volume of inputs of land, labor, and capital and in the efficiency with which they were used—increases, that is to say, in factor inputs and factor productivity. Gallman defines "labor" as the number of agricultural workers, "land" as the value of both improved and unimproved land in farms, and "capital" as the value of farm structures (houses, barns, fences, etc.), equipment, and crop and livestock inventories. Increases in these factor inputs are estimated by Gallman to have contributed slightly more than two and one-half percentage points per year (2.51%) to the annual rate of growth of agricultural output (3.11%). The contribution of total factor productivity, which is what is left ("the residual") when one subtracts the contribution of the inputs (i.e., 3.11% minus 2.51%), thus becomes approximately one-half of one percentage point a year (.60%). This, to be sure, is a modest figure, one which amounts, roughly, to between one-fifth and one-sixth of the total output growth. Yet it is not to be disdained as negligible, particularly since Gallman believes this to have been a larger contribution to the growth of agricultural output than that made by productivity growth in the subsequent period, 1840–1900.

What were the sources of these increases in inputs in the agricultural sector? What were the sources of increased productivity? These are important questions, and if we can throw light on them we shall have succeeded in some measure in accounting for the growth of the agricultural sector between 1800–40. It will then be necessary to raise the question of what light this throws, in turn, on the growth of the total economy during the period. We shall proceed by briefly identifying the sources of increase in both inputs and productivity, next describing at greater length the historical process by which the latter made its contribution to the growth of the agricultural sector. Finally we shall inquire into the implications of these developments for the growth of the economy as a whole.

Increases in labor inputs in the agricultural sector originated primarily in the growth of the rural population. It is true that the agricultural *proportion* of the nation's total labor force fell from 82.6 percent in 1800 to 63.4 percent in 1840. But the *absolute size* of the rural population from which this labor force was drawn rose in the same interval from just under 5,000,000 to more than 15,000,000. Furthermore, shifts from subsistence to commercial farming had the effect of increasing the labor participation rate in agriculture. It was this enlarged agricultural labor force that served as the main source of increased inputs of improved land and capital. Raw land was purchased principally from the federal government under laws setting increasingly generous terms of acquisition. By 1832 a minimal plot of forty acres could be purchased for just $50. Farm families then proceeded to improve at least part of the land by felling trees and clearing out brush. Farm families were also the principal source of agricultural capital. Capital yields its services over long periods rather than short ones, so that by abstaining from immediate consumption farm families accumulated savings in the form of improved land and crop and livestock inventories, some part of which might be exchanged for the rude equipment then in use on farms. Finally, the use of farm family labor for the building of barns and other structures resulted in the accumulation of capital in those forms.

A brief discussion of the role of technological change is appropriate as we begin our inquiry into the sources of the increase in productivity. In comparison with the contribution made by mechanization in the second half of the century the role of technological change in the first half was a modest, but not negligible, one. The earlier period saw the introduction first of iron and then of steel plows, the displacement of the scythe by the grain cradle, the widespread adoption of domesticated imported grasses, and a number of other improvements in methods of cultivation, varieties of crop, and strains of livestock. To the extent that these innovations improved the practices of large numbers of farmers they contributed to advances in productivity. Unfortunately, however, there is reason to believe that older and less productive techniques generally held sway during the period. While societies for the improvement of agriculture were formed, and individual leadership assumed by "gentlemen farmers" as well known as George Washington and Nicholas Biddle, these endeavors appear to have exerted little influence on general practice.

Farmers generally abandoned acres worn out by water erosion and by repeated planting of tobacco and other crops, and moved on to new soil. George Washington explained the reason for this in a letter written in 1791 to the English agricultural reformer, Arthur Young: "An English farmer must entertain a contemptible opinion of our husbandry, or a horrid idea of our lands, when he shall be informed that not more than eight or ten bushels of wheat is the yield of an acre; but . . . the aim of the farmers of this country, if they can be called farmers, is not to make the most they can from the land, which is, or has been cheap, but the most of the labour, which is dear. . . ." "Our lands," Washington averred on another occasion, "were originally very good; but use and abuse have made them quite otherwise."

As Washington's letter to Young shows, contemporaries were well aware that the factor proportions of American agriculture—abundant land and scarce labor—discouraged care in the use of land and improvement in agricultural technology. Land-intensive modes of production economized on the use of both labor and capital, which were, in contrast with the situation in England, relatively dear per unit of output. As capital accumulated, its relative cost declined, and it too could be more intensively employed in the continuing battle to save on labor, especially after growing markets and improved access to them encouraged investment. Farm equipment and tools of many kinds exemplify this employment of capital.

A second source of increased productivity arose out of the westward movement onto more fertile soils. This source must not be overemphasized, for careful studies have shown that average yields per acre of corn and wheat—the major grains—were little if any higher in the Midwest than in Pennsylvania and New York. On the other hand, yields per man were undeniably higher. Studies based on various reports and on data in the first agricultural census—that of 1840—show that total man-hour labor requirements per unit of output were substantially lower for grain production in the newly settled western regions than on farms and plantations located in the eastern seaboard states. Furthermore, cotton output per man-hour input was 37 percent higher in the Southern Delta than the weighted average figure for all cotton-producing regions of the country.

While technological change and use of fertile western soil made some contribution to productivity advance, undoubtedly its main source in this period was widening markets. It was market expansion that induced shifts from subsistence to commercial agriculture, increased the intensity and quality of the work effort, and led to improved marketing mechanisms. Behind these developments lay a series of transport improvements. Without the westward movement, however, and the population and territorial growth that fed it, these developments would not have been necessary and may never have occurred.

The westward movement during this period had a northern wing and a southern wing: the former carrying most migrants into what are now the East North-central states of Ohio, Michigan, Indiana, Illinois, and Wisconsin; the latter taking them into the East South-central states of Kentucky, Tennessee, Alabama, and Mississippi. At first the movement was slow, the census for 1800 recording fewer than 400,000 inhabitants in the area west of the Appalachians. Thereafter the tide of migrants began to flow more rapidly, and by 1810 there were a million people in the region. This early population growth was of limited significance to the rest of the nation. Large numbers of people in the West lived at the level of subsistence or close to it, and while some were able to produce more than was required by consumption needs and to exchange the surplus for goods provided by wandering peddlers or nearby country stores, many represented an underemployed economic resource. As late as 1851 a western newspaper characterized as follows a settler on backlands inaccessible to markets: "He fills up his leisure time by hunting, loses his regular habits, and discouraged and disappointed, ends by doing the little that he had to do to sustain his family, in a slovenly and imperfect manner." The value of produce received at New Orleans, the port through which much of the trade of the West passed, was $5,370,000 in 1807, and it had risen only to $8,773,000 by 1816. Those other evidences of expanding trade—flourishing towns and cities—were conspicuously few. In 1810, New Orleans, with a population of 24,562, was the only city of any considerable size in the West. Pittsburgh had 4,768 inhabitants; Lexington, 4,326; and Cincinnati, 2,540. Louisville, St. Louis, Nashville, and Natchez each had fewer than 1,000.

A principal deterrent to the growth of the West before the end of the War of 1812 was the high cost of transportation for the commodities of the region. The wheat, flour, butter, pork, tobacco, hemp, lead, and other products of the rich agricultural lands of the Ohio Valley were of low value in relation to their bulk. Because of this, it was cheaper to ship them more than 3,000 miles by water—down the Ohio and Mississippi rivers to New Orleans, then up the Atlantic coast to Philadelphia, New York, or Boston—then 300 miles overland across the Appalachian highlands to Philadelphia or Baltimore.

Traffic, moreover, was for the most part a one-way flow—downriver—for shipments upriver against the current were almost prohibitively expensive. Textiles, hardware, hats, tea, and other commodities of high value relative to their bulk were imported from across the Appalachians rather than brought up the river. This was in the main another one-way flow of goods (one of the chief exceptions being cattle driven on foot over the mountains to the East Coast). This difficult pattern of interregional trade encouraged self-sufficiency rather than commercial agriculture, and depressed farm incomes in the West, as well as making western food and raw materials more expensive in the East.

The appearance of steamboats on the rivers of the West after the War of 1812 marked the beginnings of significant change in the region's pattern of economic life. In 1817 only 17 steamboats plied the western rivers, and the total volume was merely 3,290 tons; by 1840 these figures had increased phenomenally to 536 vessels and 83,592 tons. Steamboats made possible much more upriver traffic and reduced shipping costs both up and downstream. The reduction in upriver freight rates, far greater than cuts in downstream charges, lowered the costs of imported merchandise. This in turn shifted the "terms of trade" in favor of the farmer. In other words it lowered the prices of goods the farmers bought relative to those they sold. The net effect was to increase western farm incomes substantially and to encourage both an increase in the settlement of the West and a shift from subsistence to commercial agriculture.

The increase in settlement is evident from the following table, which shows population growth in the new western states between 1810 and 1840.

Table 1-1
Population Change in New Western States, 1810–40

	1810	1840
Ohio (1803)	230,760	1,519,467
Louisiana (1812)	76,556	352,411
Indiana (1816)	24,520	685,866
Mississippi (1817)	40,352	375,651
Illinois (1818)	12,282	476,183
Alabama (1819)	*	590,756
Missouri (1821)	20,845	383,702
Arkansas (1836)	1,062	97,574
Michigan (1837)	4,762	212,267

*Not available

The proportion of the total United States population living in the West rose from one-seventh in 1810 to more than one-third in 1840.

Steamboats do not deserve all the credit for the increase; for turnpikes, canals, and railroads also improved the internal conditions of the country, making the West more attractive to settlers. However, before 1840 the amount of traffic carried by railroads was negligible in comparison with that moving on all inland waterways. As we shall see, it was especially in the 1850s that railroads exerted an important influence upon the agriculture of the West. The direct influence of turnpikes was lessened by their inability to provide a cheap means of transportation over considerable distances. Like the canals, turnpikes proved to be feeders rather than competitors of steamboats. In the judgment of George R. Taylor, the steamboat was "the most important agency of internal transportation in the country" until the 1850s, when the railroad became a serious rival.

Yet canals exerted a significant impact upon the volume of agricultural production even when serving as feeders. They did so by lowering the overland freight charges made by wagon transport, their most direct competitor. Between 1800 and 1819, the ton-mile rate for carriage by wagon appears to have varied between 30 and 70 cents, rates which discouraged the long-distance shipment of bulky agricultural commodities of low value. By the 1850s, 15 cents per ton-mile appears to have been the usual rate on ordinary highways. Particular canals effected even more dramatic reductions. In 1817, the average rate for freight shipments between Buffalo and New York, via overland wagon and the Hudson River, was 19.12 cents per ton-mile. After the completed Erie Canal linked these two cities in 1825 the rate fell to an average of only 1.68 cents per ton-mile during the years 1830–50, a decline of more than 90 percent.

At first the impact of the Erie on agriculture was largely confined to the farms of western New York, but after the mid-1830s the bulky products of the West began to flow directly eastward. The effects on manufactures were also spectacular. Already by 1836 the reverse flow of manufactured products to the West amounted to nearly $10 million—a figure that was to rise sensationally to more than $94 million by 1853. As we shall see later, it is extremely probable that transport improvements helped raise personal incomes in the West even before 1840, thus enabling that region to serve as an increasingly important market for the manufactured products of the East. At the same time, rising personal incomes in the East permitted that region to enlarge its demand for the agricultural products of the West. Subsequent construction of midwestern canals, and of railroads in the 1850s, was to strengthen these interregional bonds and greatly increase the value of the goods shipped in both directions. The volume of western products shipped down the Mississippi River and its tributaries to New Orleans also increased during these years, indeed virtually doubling every decade between 1810 and 1860. Lead from Missouri, Illinois, and Wisconsin; wheat, flour, butter, pork, and pork products from western Pennsylvania, Ohio, and Indiana; and tobacco and hemp from Kentucky were among these products. But the most important of them all was cotton, and it is to the story of its appearance on the commercial stage that we must now briefly turn.

It was cotton that led the southern wing of the westward movement. Its rise to commercial prominence was a "supply response" to demands set in motion by the beginnings of the Industrial Revolution in England. During the course of the eighteenth and early nineteenth centuries a series of technological innovations in spinning and weaving and in the generation of power (the steam engine) transformed the manufacture of cotton textiles. While power spinning and weaving were only rarely brought together under the same roof to constitute factory production—in contrast with subsequent American methods—mechanization did enlarge greatly both the output of yarn and cloth, and the demand for the raw cotton essential to the production of this output. The result was an increase in the production and export of cotton to England from the numerous countries in the world whose climatic and other conditions were favorable to its growth. India, Brazil, and other countries increased their cotton output, but the American South emerged as the principal source of supply.

At first the American product consisted of "Sea Island" cotton, the culture of which had been introduced by planters along the Georgia-Carolina coast about 1786. Unlike "Uplands" cotton—the second of the two varieties grown in the United States—the fibers of Sea Island cotton were easily detachable from the seed by squeezing it between a pair of simple rollers. Silky, strong, long-fibered, and more valuable than Uplands, Sea Island cotton could only be grown in a strip thirty or forty miles wide along the coast of Carolina and Georgia that had a particularly equable climate. In consequence, exports of this variety never amounted to as much as 16 million pounds in any year prior to 1860.

The problem was different in the case of Uplands cotton: it could be extensively grown provided only that some mechanical way be found to cut the labor cost of separating its short fibers from the sticky green seeds. The invention of the cotton gin by Eli Whitney in 1793 provided the answer to this need. The gin was a simple device, a cylinder fitted with wire teeth. The latter drew the seed cotton through a wire screen that separated the seed from the lint, and a revolving brush then removed the lint from the teeth of the cylinder. Before its invention a good hand took a day to clean one pound of cotton; the gin enabled him to increase his output fifty times. And because the very simplicity of the gin made it a device that was easily imitable, a number of models soon appeared in the South. Had Whitney and his partner Phineas Miller been able to secure their patent against infringement the spread of cotton culture might have been delayed.

In possession of a favorable climate, abundant supplies of cheap and richly productive land, and an expandable plantation-labor system with which to work it, the South soon saw cotton establish a comparative advantage over most alternative crops in the regions suited to its growth. Sugar, tobacco, and rice continued to be important crops in local areas on the fringes of the Cotton Kingdom, but neither they nor any other crop succeeded in challenging the sway of the ruling staple. The cultivation of rice could not be greatly expanded because it was confined to the marshlands along the Carolina and Georgia coasts that could be drained, diked, and flooded. Requirements of soil and climate confined sugar to a small area. Wheat did not do well in the lower South. The indigo industry of the Carolinas and Georgia all but died out when the Revolution ended the bounty of six pence per pound that the British had paid. As for tobacco, according to Ulrich B. Phillips, that industry was entering in 1783 "upon a half century of such wellnigh constant low prices that the opening of each new tract for culture was offset by the abandonment of an old one, and the export remained stationary at a little less than half a million hogsheads."

In contrast with these other commercial crops, cotton became the great staple of an ever-widening portion of the southern landscape. In 1790 its growth was largely confined to a few islands off the South Carolina and Georgia coast and a few favored areas on the mainland within a few miles of the sea. With the invention of the gin, cultivation moved into the backcountry of Georgia, where, with Augusta as center and chief market, it soon covered the upland parts of that state and South Carolina. For more than a quarter of a century this was the principal cotton-producing area of the nation. Indeed, as late as 1821 more than one-half of the entire cotton crop was grown in these two states alone.

The first shift from its original center took the cotton belt north into North Carolina and Virginia and west over the mountains into Tennessee. Following the War of 1812, the decisive movement was to the Southwest, with the tide of cultivation flowing first into Alabama, Mississippi, and Louisiana, and eventually into Arkansas and Texas. By the mid-1820s South Carolina and Georgia had begun to lose their original dominant position; by the time of the Civil War they accounted for less than a quarter of the nation's cotton output. Mississippi and Alabama had become the leading states, with Louisiana not far behind. New Orleans—the great central market for the cotton of the western region—had received only 37,000 bales in 1816; but in 1822 the number was 161,000, in 1830, 428,000, and in 1840, 923,000 bales.

Expressed in terms of changing proportions, the states and territories from Alabama and Tennessee westward increased their share of the nation's total output from one-sixteenth in 1811, to one-third in 1820, one-half before 1830, and nearly two-thirds in 1840. National output rose a hundredfold between 1790 and 1820—from 3,000 bales to 335,000—and then quadrupled to 1,348,000 bales by 1840. In 1791 cotton production in the United States had represented less than one-half of one percent of world output. By 1840, 62.6 percent, or nearly two out of every three bales produced in the world, originated in this country.

Thus far we have concentrated on the production of cotton and other agricultural commodities and have said nothing about the ways in which they were marketed. Yet it seems obvious that the vast increases in output must have brought about changes in the existing methods of marketing. These had developed in response to the need to distribute far smaller quantities of goods, and they could no longer serve when volume grew far beyond the original amount. Since such changes introduced greater efficiency into the distribution process they must also have saved resources—that is, enabled a bushel of wheat or a bale of cotton to move from farm or plantation into the hands of processors at some lesser cost per unit of marketing output. Admittedly, it would be extremely difficult to measure the amount of this saving. But if a plausible argument can be made for its existence, it will be evident that the marketing sector of the economy must have made some contribution, however small, to increased productivity in the agricultural sector.

We can best clarify the development of the distribution network if we concentrate on the grain trade of the Old Northwest—an area bounded by the Ohio and Mississippi rivers—and on the cotton trade of the South. In the early years of the nineteenth century the former was in what John G. Clark has called its "pioneer stage," a stage in which "many farmers had no way of marketing their crops except to take their own shipments of produce downstream and dispose of their goods personally at some market along the river or at New Orleans." Farmers themselves owned many of the 3,000 to 4,000 flatboats which descended the rivers of the West each year. Their journeys often originated on streams too shallow for navigation by steamboats and terminated when the head of steamboat navigation was reached on a larger river. At that point, the goods were reloaded on steamboats, with the farmer himself accompanying them to market or consigning them to an agent, often the steamboat captain, for sale.

Numerous farmers were unwilling or unable to engage personally in the marketing of their crops at points distant from home. Not only would time be lost from farm work, especially at spring planting, but markets were often glutted and prices depressed, a disadvantage for the farmer in need of a quick return in order to purchase goods required at home. In these circumstances, as population increased and inland towns sprang up, country merchants appeared on the scene. Opening stores in settled communities, they bartered dry goods (cloth, thread, ready-made clothing, buttons, trimmings, etc.), hardware, and other merchandise for produce. They disposed of the latter by transporting it to a major local market such as Cincinnati or St. Louis, selling or consigning it for shipment to New Orleans, or taking it to that city themselves.

As the volume of produce to be handled increased, marketing mechanisms became more specialized. Forwarding and commission houses opened for business along the Mississippi and Ohio rivers and handled grain for both farmers and merchants. They provided storage facilities, located the most efficient transportation, and endeavored to sell in the dearest market. When country merchants consigned produce to them for sale they advanced a portion of its value in cash, enabling the merchant in turn to offer increased credit to farmers. Commission merchants (factors) in New Orleans made similar advances on consignments, thus serving as the fountainhead for a stream of credit flowing via forwarding and commission houses to country merchants and farmers. According to Clark, during the 1830s and early 1840s the financial resources of New Orleans were able to help finance the movement of produce from the Ohio valley and upper Mississippi. With the development of such grain markets as Chicago and Milwaukee in the 1850s, however, New Orleans "no longer held the lead in providing the credit necessary to draw to itself the produce of the Old Northwest."

Grain was not nearly so important an export crop as cotton—indeed, only 4 percent of the products of northern farms were exported as late as 1870—and for this reason the sources of credit that helped move it to market were overwhelmingly domestic. In the case of cotton,

English and northern capital provided most of the financing, so that the network of credit stretched all the way from London and Liverpool to farmers and planters in the American South. The marketing intermediaries were similar to those which had developed in the grain trade. In the pioneer stage of the cotton trade some farmers and planters hauled their crops to the coast and supervised their sale themselves. Village storekeepers served as outlets for remotely located farmers. As production mounted in the interior, increasing numbers of inland factors (commission merchants) settled in such fall-line towns as Augusta, Macon, Atlanta, Montgomery, Nashville, Memphis, and Shreveport and provided storage and forwarding services as well as credit to farmers and planters entrusting crops to their care. Inland factors, in turn, principally consigned the cotton to factors in the coastal cities of Charleston, Savannah, Mobile, and New Orleans.

Most factors operated from the coastal ports, especially those on the Gulf of Mexico, where the bulk of the cotton sales were made to agents or resident partners of northern or European merchants and manufacturers. Like forwarding and commission merchants handling grain, and like factors handling such other southern staples as sugar, rice, and tobacco, the cotton factor was a specialist. There had been little specialization in evidence in the coastal cities in 1800 because of the comparatively small volume of commodities handled by any one firm. Each dealer was a jack-of-all-trades selling goods of many kinds because he could not make a living by concentrating on just one.

The degree of specialization, as Adam Smith pointed out, depends on the volume of demand for a good or service. It was precisely the surging output of cotton, sugar, and other staples that created the demand for the services of the specialist, the factor who could finance a strategy of storing and waiting before selling in order to obtain better prices and who could convert his superior sources of market information into judgments concerning where and when to sell. As Harold D. Woodman has expressed it, "A factor was expected to have the skill, experience, and sources of information that would make his judgment superior to that of the planter." In contrast, farmers who had accompanied their goods to market in the pioneer stage had been unable to avoid the unfavorable supply and price conditions that often greeted them upon their arrival.

Information is not a free good: it belongs among the operating costs of business. For the farmer-gone-to-market those costs were paid in the value of time consumed, as well as in low prices and profit margins. Specialization by factors developed expertise in the performance of marketing services and reduced the cost of those services below those paid by alternative marketing methods. In sum, the commission, storage, insurance, and interest charges paid to factors by farmers and planters were less than the costs previously sustained; and it is for this reason that improved techniques in the marketing sector contributed to the growth of productivity in the agricultural sector.

We must now confront the larger question of the impact of the growth of gross farm output on the per capita output of the entire economy during this period. This is a question, let it be said at once, that is extremely difficult to answer for many reasons, not the least of which is our inability at present to say whether or not measured economic growth took place at all between 1800 and 1840! While we have Gallman's rough estimates for agriculture, we are lacking in estimates for manufacturing, transport, and other sectors of the economy. Yet, given the dominant position of agriculture throughout this period, it follows that if an increase in the rate of overall per capita output growth did take place, agriculture must have made the most important contribution to it. We return to the question with which we began: Did economic growth take place in this period? And our present answer must be that we do not know.

Yet we are not debarred by our ignorance from reaching a tentative conclusion by means of inference. Indeed, we are compelled to do so because the existence of better data after 1840 enables us to say that between the mid-1840s and mid-1850s the rate of growth of national product, to cite Gallman's words, was "unusually high." How is this phenomenon to be explained? One possibility is that the long-term (secular) growth rate suddenly accelerated, in other words, that the period was one of abrupt transition from earlier years of slower growth, with the basic cause of the shift being an increase in the pace of industrialization. This is a view favored by Walt W. Rostow, who regards the 1840s as the period of the economy's "takeoff" into modern economic growth. Paul A. David disagrees. After making an effort to reconstruct the fragmentary remains of the "statistical dark age," David has concluded that the secular growth rate was not substantially lower before 1840 than afterward. He does not deny that an acceleration of the rate occurred after the mid-1840s. He simply maintains that this was a near-term rather than a long-term affair, and that it was only the latest of a series of bursts in acceleration that took place in the antebellum period. These bursts or surges are characteristic of "long-swings" or growth cycles—periods of 15-20 years in duration—in which growth at an accelerated rate is followed by growth at a declining rate.

David has traced three long-swings between the 1790s and outbreak of the Civil War, and has identified the periods of surge within each of them. In the first long-swing, the surge covered the years from the early 1790s to about 1806 and is clearly associated with a great expansion in the volume of foreign trade, especially of the carrying trade, an expansion that arose out of profit-making opportunities presented to American neutral shipping during the wars of the French Revolution. In the second long-swing the surge lasted from the early 1820s to about 1834 and seems connected with early manufacturing development. The 1820s witnessed rapid growth in a number of manufacturing industries; for example, iron making, woolen goods, carpets, paper, flint glass, lead, sugar and molasses, and salt. Factory consumption of wool rose from 400,000 pounds in 1810 to 15,000,000 in 1830, with fully half the increase falling between 1816 and 1830. Carpet production grew from an output of 9,984 yards in 1810 to 1,147,500 in 1834, with most of the increase taking place during a four-or-five year period beginning in 1827. The output of cotton textiles grew especially rapidly in the 1820s. The period of surge in the third long-swing, also apparently associated with continuing industrialization, commenced in the latter half of the 1840s and ran its course before the firing on Fort Sumter. None of these surges, it should be emphasized once more, involved a break in the secular rate of growth. There was near-term but not long-term acceleration.

At the present moment a choice between the takeoff and the long-swing hypotheses cannot conclusively be made on the basis of historical evidence. It is true that Gallman, in a critique of some of David's assumptions and estimates, has ventured a "guess" that acceleration did take place very gradually over a "very extended period of time," and that no "abrupt transition" from low to high rates of change occurred in the 1840s and 1850s. In an even more recent publication, he has adopted the position that per capita product before 1840 was "probably increasing at a rising rate." But we do not yet know the degree of this rise nor the length of time over which it extended. Until we do, uncertainty must remain about the angle of abruptness marking the transition of the forties.

Nevertheless, even if the statistical evidence, when in, should indicate a steep ascent to a higher growth path in the forties, historians are far more likely to look with favor upon David's long-swing hypothesis than upon Rostow's takeoff. Most students of our economic history, indeed of history generally, find it difficult to believe in the existence of discontinuous shifts. They believe the terminology of takeoff misleading in its implications that an economy moves from one discrete stage to another and that the defining characteristics of a given stage are readily identifiable and separable from those of another. They emphasize the overlappings between past and present, and the gradualness with which economic and social structures undergo fundamental change. Furthermore, they recognize that the effects of developments that enhance the efficiency of productive effort are not felt everywhere at once. These developments make their way with varying rates of speed through the geographic regions, sectors, industries, and firms of which an economy is composed. Sometimes they encounter opposition from firms desiring to protect older techniques imbedded in investment. Sometimes mere slowness of entrepreneurial imagination is at work. And sometimes insufficient or inadequate printed media for the dissemination of information on new techniques slows the process of diffusion. Change in the rate of growth reflects substantial change in the quantity or quality of productive inputs, and this is a process that takes time.

These reflections and presently available evidence dispose us to side with Gallman's view that the rate of growth accelerated very gradually over a very extended part of the antebellum period and that the quickened pace of industrialization in the 1840s and 1850s generated a long-swing surge rather than a fundamental shift in the trend of growth. Certainly this hypothesis of slow and gradual change is congenial with one's expectations from an economy dominated by agriculture and would appear to justify our emphasis on the importance of the productivity-enhancing developments within and adjacent to that sector. However, we must now confront more directly the evidence for industrialization during the years before 1840 and inquire into its possible effects on the pace of economic change.

Between 1810 and 1840 workers in agriculture fell from 83.7 percent of the labor force to 63.4 percent, while those in factory production rose from 3.2 percent to 8.8 percent. Since labor productivity was lowest in agriculture and highest in manufacturing, one might be tempted to credit the latter sector with the greater contribution to productivity growth. However, to do so would be a mistake because in 1840 income earned in manufacturing was not only small in relation to agriculture, it also amounted to little more than a quarter of total *nonagricultural* income. It should be emphasized that the manufacturing sector was very small in 1840 and that even the high rates of change in that decade represent small absolute increases. Gallman himself has concluded that productivity growth in nonagriculture before 1840 "must have been dominated by experience in nonmanufacturing activities, specifically, by experience in construction and the services." Significantly, he adds that there is "no reason to suppose that productivity in these activities grew as fast as productivity in agriculture." Once more, our emphasis on developments which enhanced the productivity of agriculture would appear justified.

There is an additional reason to discount the relative importance of manufacturing before approximately the mid-1830s. In manufacturing it was particularly the advent of the factory system with its "battery of machines operated from a single source of power," and its "large permanent work force whose tasks were subdivided and routinized" that made possible economies of scale and enhanced the productivity of labor. Yet as late as 1832, as is clear from a detailed report on American manufactures made that year to Louis McLane, secretary of the treasury, large factories—those with assets of $100,000 or more, or those with 250 or more workers—were overwhelmingly concentrated in only one area, the textile industry. Since the progressive enlargement of a manufacturing sector more and more dominated by the factory system is bound to have made contributions to growth of increasing significance in later years, the origins of the system deserve more than a passing word.

In the United States, as in England, it was mechanized production of cotton textiles that wrote the preface to the Industrial Revolution. Before 1812 mechanical methods were applied only to the production of thread in spinning mills; after 1817, when the power loom was introduced, both power spinning and weaving were increasingly integrated under the same factory roof. The early growth of the textile industry had been favored by the protection from British imports afforded by the Embargo, the Nonintercourse acts, and war; but the renewal of British competition after the War of 1812 snuffed out most of these enterprises. Nevertheless, development was remarkably rapid following the industry's recovery from this blow. The number of spindles in cotton mills, a mere 5,000 in 1805, had risen to more than 100,000 in 1815; they then rose once again to over 1,000,000 in 1831. By 1840 the rising textile industry of the United States was consuming well over 100,000,000 pounds of cotton a year, approximately 20 percent of total American output.

While substantial development occurred in the Middle Atlantic states, and to a limited extent also in the South and West, the major part of this growth took place in New England. According to the estimates of Robert B. Zevin, the output of cotton cloth in New England rose from less than 4,000,000 yards in 1817 to 323,000,000 in 1840. Output was increasingly the product of large-scale factories. In 1816 such factories had employed only about 5,000 people, roughly 1 percent of the region's labor force. In contrast, in 1840 about 100,000, roughly one-seventh of the labor force, were so employed. Some factories employed up to 1,500 workers each! In addition, smaller factories existed at hundreds of New England's water-power sites. Such large cities as Lowell and Holyoke were created entirely by the surge in industrial activity.

Urban workers consumed as well as produced manufactured goods, and some idea of the increasing importance of this segment of demand is supplied by the fact that between 1790 and 1840 the urban proportion of the population increased from 5 percent to 10.8 percent. Indeed, urban demand, together with the demand of the growing population of the West, helped unleash the great surge in output of cotton cloth in New England, especially during the period 1816–33. Garments made of cotton were increasingly preferred to those made of wool, for the latter were irritating to the skin, uncomfortably warm in summer, and difficult to clean. Styles in women's clothing also swelled the demand as the number of petticoats required by fashion multiplied and their circumference widened. Despite the increased demand, however, textile prices fell substantially more than other commodity prices did—that of ordinary sheeting, for example, declining from 30 cents a yard in about 1816 to 6½ cents by 1843. What made these price declines possible was a combination of factors: better textile machinery, especially Francis Cabot Lowell's improvement of the power loom, which cut wage costs; a fall in the price of raw cotton; and growth in the number of skilled technicians.

This latter factor would prove increasingly important in the decades ahead, for the diffusion of technological advance required increases in both the number and quality of skilled workers. Fortunately, the country appears to have had a large native pool of skills on which to draw. The fact that Lowell, as well as his predecessors in textile machinery development, could find skilled native workmen to assist them is, in the words of George S. Gibb, "attributable to the training of many generations of farmer-mechanics in the workshops of colonial New England." "Varied and dextrous mechanical abilities," Gibb adds, "were all but universal. . . . " Skilled craftsmen among immigrants supplemented this stock of human capital, but its main source was the native population. And while formal education, especially at the primary level, helped in the acquisition of mechanical skills, their main source was on the job training. Americans learned most by doing. Once more, this capability would have an even greater significance in the decades ahead, when factory production of an increasing number of goods would widen the swath being cut through the economy by the process of industrialization.

TWO

The Challenge of Industry, 1840–1860

In the final two decades of the antebellum era the population of the United States nearly doubled in size, rising from 17 million to 31 million. Natural increase—the excess of births over deaths—was the main source of growth, and this is true despite a falling white birthrate, which declined steadily each decade from 55.0 per thousand in 1800 to 41.4 in 1860. Immigration was also an important factor during these years. In contrast to the period between the end of the revolutionary war and 1819, when only 250,000 persons are estimated to have migrated to the United States, and to the years between 1820–40, when new immigrants are estimated at 700,000, the net figure for 1840–60 is 4,200,000!

People who leave their native land do so for many reasons, some of which impel, others of which induce them to go. Since impelling forces vary from one country to the next, and from time to time, it may at first glance seem difficult to explain in any simple way the timing of immigration to the United States in the nineteenth century. In fact, however, immigration statistics closely coincide with the long-swings in economic activity whose existence we noted in the last chapter. It was above all the surging prosperity phases of these long-swings that induced migration. In general, Europeans sought jobs, opportunities for material betterment.

Immigrants from some countries, however, did respond to pushing factors at particular times. In the period of our present concern, the Irish potato famine of the 1840s helps account for the concentration of the bulk of the arrivals in the decade 1846–55. Even then, though, sizable numbers of people also entered the country from Germany and Great Britain, and numerous Irishmen must also have responded to the promise of American life. In a word, the pull of a burgeoning economy, must be given its considerable due, as well as pushing factors on the European side.

Once again, the studies of Robert E. Gallman provide our best view of the condition of the economy during these years. One way to measure economic growth is to estimate the value added to raw materials by productive activity. Gallman's estimates of value added by commodity production in agriculture, mining, construction, and manufacturing between 1839–59 are shown in Table 2-1. Estimates are in constant prices (i.e., in dollars of constant purchasing power), and the figures therefore represent changes in real output.

Table 2-1
Value Added by Commodity Output, 1839–59 (in 1879 prices)

	Output (billions of $)	*Output per capita*	*Output per worker*
1839	$1,094	$64	$244
1844	1,374	68	*
1849	1,657	71	268
1854	2,317	85	*
1859	2,686	85	330

*Not available

Even more recently, Gallman has shown the rate of growth of the Gross National Product (GNP) during overlapping decades of the same period.

Decades	*GNP*	*GNP per capita*
1834–43 to 1844–53	51%	11%
1839–48 to 1849–58	65	22

However we display the growth, Gallman's estimates disclose an acceleration in its rate between 1839–59. Yet it will bear repeating that we do not know whether the acceleration represents an interruption in the long-term trend of growth (i.e., a takeoff) or is a more abbreviated period of surge occurring in the course of a long-swing. Nor are the causes of the acceleration clear. Was it due to an increase in the rate of capital formation, especially in manufacturing? To an improvement in the quality of land as the frontier moved west? To the impact of technological innovation upon the efficiency with which labor, capital, and land were used? To such questions as these we may now turn.

Ideally, we should be able to indicate the rates at which supplies of land, labor, and capital increased during the last two decades before the war, and also the rate at which the measured productivity of these factors increased. Unfortunately, we are lacking in such estimates. We do know that the labor force approximately doubled in these two decades, rising from 5,660,000 to 11,110,000 persons. Because immigrants contributed to this increase it would be desirable to know more than we do about the relationship between immigration and economic growth. It seems clear that immigrants contributed to growth in two ways: (1) by supplying human capital—embodying both formal and informal training—paid for by the country of origin, which also paid maintenance costs in the unproductive period of youth; and (2) by introducing new methods, information concerning which would otherwise have been obtainable only at substantial cost, if at all. Unfortunately, the subject has been insufficiently examined. Yet while it is probably safe to assume that immigrants had only trivial amounts of formal schooling, they were mainly young adults whose practical experience as farmers and artisans must have made innumerable unrecorded contributions to improved methods of production. Ideally, we should be fully informed concerning the nature of these contributions to specific industries in particular times and places, and hopefully scholars will soon begin to investigate in a systematic way the effects of immigrant knowledge and skills, attitudes and values, on productivity. Hopefully, too, they will also inquire into the differential impact of various ethnic and national groups.

It is only relatively recently that questions concerning the impact of education on *native* workers have begun to be raised. Society's investment in education was certainly small. If one adds direct expenditures to earnings from employment foregone by students while enrolled in school, the total investment in 1860 amounts to less than 1.5 percent of the national product. Aggregate figures, however, do not reveal regional differences, and in this case these are of critical importance. According to Albert Fishlow, as early as 1790 nearly everyone in New England possessed a common school education, while in the middle states "very few freeborn illiterates" were to be found. In the South, in contrast, only a few public schools existed, and education was confined largely to the wealthier classes. It is important to keep in mind, however, that the comparatively small amount of industrial, commercial, and urban growth in the South, together with the existence of slavery, which tended to depress the wages and threaten the social position of free labor, restricted employment opportunities in that region. In consequence, the great bulk of the free labor force was concentrated in the very regions where state laws provided for the education of children in the rudiments of knowledge.

While we are justified in concluding that the nation's

free labor force was widely literate, the chances are that workers knew little more than how to read, write, and figure. Fishlow estimates that the generation attending school in 1800 received on the average only 210 days of education in their entire lives, although this statistic more than doubled between 1800 and 1850. Little as this seems, it is nevertheless true that in 1850 the American figures for school enrollments were the highest in the world. The limited instruction obtained must be set alongside the comparatively undeveloped body of technological knowledge in existence. There was little reason for its conceptualization and distribution. As before, on the job training provided the expertise that workers required.

While we cannot estimate rates of increase for factor inputs and their measured productivity during these two decades, we can speak more confidently when we inquire into the effects of change in the structure of the labor force upon the productivity of labor. Between 1840–60 the agricultural portion continued its decline and the manufacturing portion its relative rise. While agricultural workers increased in absolute numbers from 3,570,000 to 5,880,000, they declined as a percentage of the total labor force from 63.4 percent to 53.2 percent. The numbers in factory production rose from 500,000 to 1,530,000; as a percentage of the total, workers in factory manufacturing and construction increased from 13.9 percent to 18.5 percent. If we keep in mind that labor productivity was in general considerably lower in agriculture than in manufacturing, it will be clear that this structural shift, decreasing as it did the numbers of workers in the sector of relatively low productivity and increasing the number in that of high productivity, contributed significantly to an increase in the productivity of the labor force as a whole.

There are three additional reasons for stressing the importance to growth of advances on the manufacturing front in this period. As Table 2-2 shows, agriculture's share in value added by commodity output declined from 72 percent in 1839 to 56 percent in 1859, while the share of manufacturing rose from 17 percent to 32 percent.

Table 2-2
Sector Shares in Value Added by Commodity Output

	Agriculture	Mining	Manufacturing	Construction
1839	72%	1%	17%	10%
1844	69	1	21	9
1849	60	1	30	9
1854	57	1	29	13
1859	56	1	32	11

Urbanization also attests to the relative decline of the farming population, and during this period the urban proportion of the total population increased significantly from 10.8 percent in 1840 to 19.8 percent in 1860. Finally, we need to take into account changes in relative per capita income between 1840–60: As Table 2-3 shows, it was only in the Northeast that an increase occurred.* The

---

*It should be emphasized that the regional comparisons shown in this table pertain only to *relative* income. In absolute terms, per capita income probably rose in the South, perhaps substantially.

share of the South fell, while that of the North-central region remained unchanged. And it was precisely in the Northeast that manufacturing was concentrated. In 1850 that region accounted for three-fourths of the nation's manufacturing employment, and in 1860 the percentage was still 71 percent. In a word, it is unmistakably clear that manufacturing activity provides the main explanation of interregional differences in income.

Table 2-3
Personal Income per Capita in Each Region As Percentage of United States Average, 1840–60

Regions	1840	1860
United States	100	100
Northeast	135	139
New England	132	143
Middle Atlantic	136	137
North-central states	68	68
East North-central	67	69
West North-central	75	66
South	76	72
South Atlantic	70	65
East South-central	73	68
West South-central	144	115

SOURCE: Richard A. Easterlin, in Seymour E. Harris, ed., *American Economic History* (New York: McGraw-Hill, 1961), p. 528. Copyright 1961 by McGraw-Hill Book Company and used by permission.

These structural shifts in commodity and income shares and in urbanization provide valuable indices of the nature and direction of change in the antebellum economy. Manufacturing served as the cutting edge of growth, and this warrants our emphasis upon its importance. At the same time, emphasis must be applied judiciously, and the strongly supportive role of agriculture not be overlooked. There are good reasons for taking a balanced view. For one thing, as a glance at Table 2-2 will disclose, the changes in the shares of agriculture and manufacturing in commodity output are far more marked in the 1840s than in the 1850s: if the manufacturing sector supplied the cutting edge of growth, its blade got duller instead of sharper as the forties gave way to the fifties. For another, a comparison of Tables 2-1 and 2-2 will reveal that in the very period—1849–54—when per capita output made its sharpest ascent (from $71 to $85), value added by commodity output in manufacturing actually *declined* (from 30% to 29%). Finally, if one looks at the ratio of fixed reproducible capital to income originating in various sectors of the economy between 1840–60, one finds the ratio in agriculture increasing from 1.2 percent to 1.7 percent, while the ratio in manufacturing and mining combined remains unchanged at .9 percent. It should be underscored, then, that in 1860 most workers continued to be employed in agriculture; it was that sector which dominated commodity output. While growing, the manufacturing sector was still small. While declining, the agricultural sector continued to be large.

The history of agriculture in this period, as before, is dominated by the continued surge of population to the

West. In 1790 almost all of the American people had lived on the East Coast; by 1860, precisely half of them inhabited either the East Central region (35%), the West Central region (13%), or the Far West (2%). (See Table 2-4.) Massive shifts of these dimensions not only altered

Table 2-4
Geographic Distribution of Population, 1790–1860

Regions	1790	1800	1810	1820	1830	1840	1850	1860
I. East Coast	97%	93%	85%	77%	71%	63%	57%	50%
A. New England	26	23	20	17	15	13	12	10
B. Middle Atlantic	24	27	28	28	28	30	25	26
C. South Atlantic	47	43	37	32	28	20	20	14
II. East Central	3	7	14	20	26	32	34	35
A. North	0	1	4	8	12	17	19	22
B. South	0	6	10	12	14	15	15	13
III. West Central	0	0	1	3	3	5	8	13
A. North	0	0	0	1	1	2	4	7
B. South	0	0	1	2	2	3	4	6
IV. Far West	0	0	0	0	0	0	1	2
Total U.S.	100	100	100	100	100	100	100	100

SOURCE: U.S. Bureau of the Census, *Historical Statistics of the United States from Colonial Times to 1957* (Washington, D. C.: Government Printing Office, 1960), pp. 12–13.

the economic prospects of the people who moved, but also the prospects of those who remained behind. Faced by competition from such prairie soils as those of Illinois, Wisconsin, and Iowa—three states whose output accounted for 45 percent of the increase in the American wheat crop between 1849–59—farmers in eastern and southern states tended to abandon wheat as a major cash crop. Some left their overcropped farms and went west; others took up cattle raising, dairy farming, and cheese making, or went into diversified types of farming. Similar phenomena were to be found in the South. In the upland areas from Virginia to Georgia, the expansion of cotton and tobacco left soil exhaustion in its wake. By 1850 a large proportion of Virginia and Maryland east of the Blue Ridge Mountains was a waste of old fields and abandoned lands. The impact of the westward movement on individuals thus varied from crop to crop and place to place, depending on the vagaries of nature, past history, markets, and technology.

Undoubtedly, the main way in which that movement influenced the growth of the economy was through its creation and development of the resources of newer agricultural regions. Abetted by transport changes and other developments to be discussed, gradual increases in output altered regional shares of the nation's personal income per capita (Table 2-3). It should again be made clear that Table 2-3 reveals relative rather than absolute changes in income, with each region's income shown as a percentage of average income in the United States as a whole. We shall illustrate the process by which the westward movement in this period brought about these changes in income shares by focusing on the development of agriculture on the western prairies, especially those of the West North-central region. While this region's rate of income growth was somewhat lower than the national average, its population, in response to the lessening of difficulties in prairie farming, was increasing more rapidly in the 1850s than that of any other region. Furthermore, the rate of income growth in the 1860 estimate reflects the inclusion of the new frontier states of Kansas, Nebraska, and Minnesota. If the rate of growth had been computed only for the states of 1840 (Missouri and Iowa), it might have compared more favorably with the national trend.

By 1860 the northern part of the western domain stretched irregularly between the Appalachian Mountains and a region of diminishing rainfall marked by the hundredth meridian. Bounded on the north by the Great Lakes and on the south by the border states, the area was principally one of lake plains or prairie plains. The former clustered about the Great Lakes; the latter began in a small way in Ohio and Michigan before marching to the horizon as they penetrated northern Indiana, central Illinois, Missouri, Iowa, and eastern Kansas. Treeless except for groves of oak, hickory, and walnut on the morainal ridges and stands of timber along the streams, the prairies were an area of extremely high fertility. The glacial ice cap had pulverized rocks into a deep and finely powdered soil rich in phosphorous, potassium, magnesium, and other chemical constituents. The rotting of the coarse, thick, and deeply penetrating root structure of the bluestem grass that covered the prairies with a luxurious growth added valuable humus to the soil. The contrast with the thin forest soils of upland New England and New York could hardly have been more marked. Blessed with an abundance of rainfall and sunshine, the area was potentially one of the richest agricultural regions of the world.

A number of obstacles, however, impeded the settlement of the prairies before the 1850s. Among these were the absence of natural drainage; the lack of timber for buildings, fences, and fuel; and the resistance of the coarse root structure to wooden moldboard and cast iron plows. Moreover, the damp and heavy prairie soils clung to the plowshare of the common sorts of plow used by the early settlers in the area. By the 1850s cast steel plows imported from England were introduced, and these combined greater smoothness in the moldboard with lightness and strength. Tiling and the construction of ditches made better drainage possible, although both were costly operations beyond the resources of men of small means. The coming of the railroad to the prairie states, finally, made it possible to bring in lumber from other regions, while the introduction of wire fencing provided material for enclosing the fields.

Partly in response to these developments, an exceptionally large amount of new land was improved for agricultural use during the 1850s. Indeed, if we compare the amount of land improved during a given decade with the amount of improved farmland in existence at the beginning of the decade, we obtain a ratio of 0.33 for the decade ending 1849, and an increase in that ratio to 0.44 for the ten years ending in 1859. That the prairie states figured substantially in this development is suggested by the fact that the West North-central region was the fastest growing part of the nation in the 1850s (see Table 2-4), with population gains in Minnesota, Iowa, Missouri, and Kansas particularly impressive.

The contribution of railroads to this growth deserves

emphasis. Admittedly, Robert Fogel is right in arguing that railroads were not indispensably necessary. Had additional canals and roads been constructed instead, they would have served as reasonably good substitutes for the fabled iron horse. Yet the historical fact remains that railroads were the chosen instruments of the times. Sparked by federal and state land grants to the Illinois Central and other prairie railroads, and encouraged by the absence of engineering difficulties on the level land, a major railroad construction boom got under way in the 1850s. During that decade mileage in Indiana, Illinois, Missouri, and Iowa increased from 339 to 6,635. Settlers did not wait upon the railroads but entered the region in anticipation of their coming—and also in anticipation of rising land and commodity prices. But initial levels of agricultural production were low except for those enjoying access to markets by water. Completion of railroad construction resulted in immediate increases in the volume of output in these areas and spread a thicker blanket of settlement and production as well. The advent of efficient transportation thus made a major contribution to the development of prairie agriculture.

In enabling the prairie land to be cleared the railroad also made possible a significant saving of the nation's resources. If the prairie states had not been settled, additional acres of the forested land of the East would have had to be cleared. The difference in cost emerges from Martin Primack's estimate that whereas $11 per acre was expended in the 1850s in preparing for cultivation 5 million acres of treeless land, the same extension on the forested land of the East would have cost $24 an acre.

Actual cultivation in the West not only saved money but labor as well. The researches of William Parker and Judith Klein have shown that both corn and wheat could be grown on western soil with smaller inputs of labor. The preharvest and harvest operations on the corn crop of the West required only 1.81 man-hours per bushel. This compares with a national average of 3.51. For wheat, the difference is smaller—2.84 man-hours in contrast with 3.17 nationally. These measurements reflect only the smaller number of man-hours required on each acre of western soil. But there is also reason to believe that yields per acre increased as one moved west onto virgin soils with the accumulated fertility of centuries.

In sum, agricultural productivity increased in the prairie states because of the advent of the railroad, the lower cost of readying open lands for cultivation, and the somewhat superior yields of western soils. To these sources of greater efficiency we must now add the contribution made not only to prairie farming but to agriculture generally by better machinery. The beginnings of technological improvement in agriculture go back to the early nineteenth century; but such innovations as Jethro Wood's iron plow (1819), steel plows adapted to tough prairie soils (1830s), harrows and seed drills (1840s), and corn planters (1850s) exerted only limited impact because relatively few of these farm implements were manufactured and sold commercially. In the 1850s, however, real farm gross output increased considerably, and in the decade 1855–65 the annual rate of real investment in implements and farm machinery rose to $23 million, more than double that of the preceding decade. By 1857 John

Deere was turning out 10,000 plows a year, while as early as 1851 Cyrus McCormick was making 1,000 mechanical reapers a year in his Chicago factory. The contribution of the reaper to labor productivity may be seen in the following estimate by Leo Rogin: a man with a sickle could cut one-half to three-quarters of an acre of wheat in a day; with a cradle he could cut two to three acres a day; and with a self-rake reaper he could cut ten to twelve acres a day.

The adoption of the reaper had a tremendous effect upon the agriculture of the Northwest. Farmers turned from corn to wheat, and wheat acreage more than doubled. A major wheat-producing center came into existence in northern Illinois and southern Wisconsin. In the years 1849–57 eleven counties in northern Illinois purchased approximately one-fourth of the total number of McCormick reapers sold. By the eve of the Civil War northern agriculture stood poised on the threshold of our first agricultural revolution. What made for revolution was the rapidity of change from manpower to horsepower. By 1860, every stage in the growing of grain was amenable to the use of horse-drawn machines.

What of the South? of slavery? of cotton? To what extent did this region and its people and products participate in the expansion that characterized northern agriculture between 1840–60? The answers to these questions may be surprising. In the first place, in the South as well as North, the rate of population increase was greater in the western parts than in the older areas. In the states of the South Atlantic region the number of people increased by less then 50 percent and in those of the East South-central region by less than 60 percent. In contrast, the increase in the West South-central states exceeded 300 percent! As in population growth, so also in output growth. Percentage increases in cotton production in the three West South-central states between 1849–59 far exceeded those of any other state. Arkansas's output rose by 524.5 percent, Louisiana's by 335.5 percent, and Texas's by a whopping 727.5 percent.

We must not permit these figures to mislead us, however. While they are truly indicative of rapid growth, we must not confuse percentage *increases* in output, which are typically high in early stages of growth, with percentages of *total* output. In 1859, the cotton crop of Texas was only 1 percent of United States production, that of Arkansas 0.8 percent, and that of Louisiana 15.4 percent. Nearly half of the total output—48.1 percent—was the product of two states of the East South-central region, Mississippi and Alabama. Georgia, an older state of the South Atlantic region, contributed an additional 15.4 percent. These are sufficient reasons for not confining our search for sources of productivity advance to any one part of the antebellum South. Rather, we must examine the Cotton Kingdom as a whole.

When we look away to Dixieland we are apt to see only vast plantations on which hundreds of slaves toiled "from day clean to first dark" to produce the South's cotton crop. To be sure, the large plantation was an essential part of the picture, but the part must not be mistaken for the whole. In 1860 there were in the South 1,516,000 free families, of whom only 385,000 were owners of slaves; nearly three-fourths of all free southern families owned no slaves at all! The typical white southerner was not only a small farmer but also a nonslave-holder. A large majority of the slave-owning families, moreover, owned only a few slaves. In 1850, as Table 2-5 reveals, 89 percent of the owners held fewer than 20 slaves; 71 percent, fewer than 10; and almost 50 percent,

Table 2-5
Percentage Distribution of Slaveholding Families According to Number of Slaves Held, 1790 and 1850

Number of Slaves	Percentage of Families	
	1790	*1850*
1	24.5	17.4
2 and under 5	30.5	29.5
5 and under 10	22.0	24.4
10 and under 20	14.3	17.4
20 and under 50	6.4	9.1
50 and under 100	1.0	1.7
100 and under 200	0.2	0.4
200 and under 300	a	0.1
300 and over	a	a
Unknown	1.0	

a = Less than one-tenth of 1 percent.
SOURCE: *Compendium of the Seventh Census* (Washington, D.C.: A. O. P. Nicholson, Public Printer, 1854), Table XC, p. 95.

fewer than 5. If we accept the usual definition of a planter as a man who owned at least 20 slaves, these proportions make it clear not only that the typical slaveholder was not a planter, but also that the typical planter worked only a moderate-sized gang of from 20 to 50 slaves. The planter aristocracy was made up of some 10,000 families living off the labor of gangs of more than 50 slaves. Yet it was on the large agricultural units that most of the slaves were to be found. Ownership was so highly concentrated that only one-fourth of the slaves belonged to masters holding fewer than 10; considerably more than half lived on plantations holding more than 20; and approximately a quarter belonged to masters owning more than 50.

As is suggested by the fact that a large majority of the owners held only a few slaves, cotton was the crop of the little man as well as the big. Indeed, its cultivation required no slave labor at all, and it was accordingly grown on small farms without slaves—or with only a few—and on middling-to-large-sized farms as well as on plantations. Unlike rice and sugarcane, which required large investments of capital for processing machinery, cotton was cheap to grow. A small farmer could cultivate it with the assistance of his wife and children, and he had little trouble getting it ginned and prepared for market. As a rule, the value of cotton in relation to its bulk was sufficiently high to bear the costs of transport over considerable distances without jeopardizing the chance of profit. Cotton stood abuse much better than many other farm commodities; it was nonperishable and hence suffered relatively little from rough handling, exposure, long delays, and poor warehousing while in transit to market. Smaller agricultural units were thus enabled to make substantial contributions to each year's crop. Nevertheless, in all probability the bulk of the crop came from the plantations, where most of the slaves were concentrated.

Modes of operation and management, which varied with the size of the agricultural units, were undoubtedly more efficient on large plantations. On small farms—the great majority of the units in the South—masters usually gave close personal supervision to the unspecialized labor of a few slaves. Many were obliged to work in the fields alongside their hands, although those owning as few as a half dozen slaves sought a more elevated social status by refraining from such labor. Small slave forces lacked skilled craftsmen, and their masters found it necessary to repair tools, do carpentry work, and perform other specialized tasks. At picking time in the fall the master usually supplemented his small force with his own labor.

Substantial farmers and small planters who owned from 10 to 30 slaves normally lived on their own land and devoted full time to the management of their enterprise. They did not as a rule employ overseers, although they might have the aid of a slave foreman or driver, whose essential function was to urge on the slave gangs by word or whip. Agricultural units of this size usually benefited from some labor specialization. Besides the field hands and driver, a few slaves might exercise manual skills or perform domestic work. Even so, the unit was too small for full-time carpenters or cooks, so that the latter often had to work in the fields as well.

Maximum specialization was possible for those planters who owned thirty or more slaves, although less than half of them appear to have used overseers. The latter were generally retained on a year-to-year basis under a written contract that could be terminated at will by either party, and as a rule each overseer made use of one or more drivers in working the slave gang. The "gang system" was one of two basic methods of labor management. Under the other—the less frequently used "task system"—each hand was given a specific daily assignment and could quit work when the task was completed. The planter who hired a full-time overseer was able to devote his own attention to problems of marketing, finance, and general plantation administration. He also enjoyed sufficient leisure to be able to absent himself from his plantation more or less at his own discretion. But absentee ownership was not characteristic on plantations of any size.

Plantations containing thirty or more slaves enjoyed a considerable degree of labor specialization. Household servants and field hands were clearly distinguished from each other, and the latter were divided between plow gangs and hoe gangs. On the larger plantations slaves were able to devote their full time to such occupations as ditching, tending livestock, driving wagons, and taking care of vegetable gardens. In 1854 one Virginia planter had 8 plowmen, 10 hoe hands, 2 wagoners, 4 oxcart drivers, a carriage driver, a hostler, a stable boy, a shepherd, a cowherd, a swineherd, 2 carpenters, 5 masons, 2 smiths, a miller, 2 shoemakers, 5 spinners, a weaver, a butler, 2 waitresses, 4 maids, a nurse, a laundress, a seamstress, a dairymaid, a gardener, and 2 cooks attached to the field service. The owner of a very large establishment employed a general manager or steward to help him run the estate. If several plantations were involved he might run one himself, but as a rule he hired an overseer for each of them.

In sum, the ability to employ specialized labor was one of the sources of the "economies of scale" possible on large plantations. And it follows from this that the westward movement, by making available cheaper land to be organized into large agricultural units, must be included among the sources of productivity growth in the Cotton Kingdom. Efforts to measure these economies, however, have not won universal scholarly approval. It seems evident that large plantations also gave rise to "diseconomies," partly in the form of losses of time in getting about, and perhaps partly also in the form of an increase in the ratio of drivers to overseers. Certainly it is plausible to assume that the larger the number of drivers, the greater the problem of supervising them and, in consequence, the greater the opportunity for slave gangs to relax the intensity of their labor. It should be noted though that there is some evidence that slaves worked more days per year and perhaps more hours per day than free farmers.

The question of the relationship between the intensity of labor and its productivity requires more systematic evidence before it can be resolved. Other kinds of evidence exist in support of the proposition that the productivity of slave labor increased in the final decade of the antebellum period. Sample studies of the manuscript schedules of the United States census indicate that cotton output per worker in the seven leading cotton states increased at an annual rate of 2.9 percent between 1849–59. This suggests that other inputs required for cotton production increased more rapidly than labor. And indeed this was the case. Improved land in use on farms in these states increased at an annual rate of 4 percent while both the slave and total populations grew at only 3 percent. Probably a disproportionately growing share of these lands was devoted to the raising of cotton. Certainly the annual output of corn, the second most important crop of the seven states, grew more slowly than that of cotton. In a word, inputs of land devoted to cotton production increased more rapidly than did labor. And probably this was land of high quality, so that this too contributed to the rising productivity of the slave labor force. Finally, an increase in capital per worker also occurred. Census estimates reveal the value of farming implements and machinery per improved acre to have been 25 percent higher in the seven leading cotton states than in the nation as a whole.

These considerations help explain the relatively high rate of growth of per capita income in the South between 1840–60. According to recent computations by Robert W. Fogel and Stanley Engerman, income grew at an average annual rate of 1.7 percent, a figure well in excess of the national average rate of 1.3 percent. This result is obtained even when slaves are included in the population count. When they are viewed as "intermediate goods," and the cost of their maintenance is therefore excluded from aggregate income, the rate of growth for free southerners becomes 1.8 percent. Furthermore, despite age-old views to the contrary, recent studies have shown that investments in slaves were profitable, yielding rates of return comparable to those obtainable from a variety of nonagricultural enterprises. If—as an older school of thought once maintained—plantation owners held slaves in order to educate them in the ways of civilized man, they were well rewarded for their nobility.

In sum, the contribution of agriculture, both northern and southern, to the growth of the American economy was a substantial one. Indeed, it was an even more substantial one than our discussion thus far of its direct contributions would lead one to believe. Agriculture also made a very important indirect contribution by supplying a land-intensive base for the rising manufacturing industries of the antebellum period. Because of the abundance and cheapness of land, raw materials were also abundant and cheap—far more so than in economies, such as the British one, in which land was relatively scarce. In the United States, capital and labor were relatively scarce and expensive, and this would have made it difficult for American manufacturers to compete with imported goods the manufacture of which entailed a lesser cost for capital and labor per unit of output. Cheaper raw materials helped overcome these advantages of foreign manufacture. In fact, it was precisely those industries processing raw materials that were the leading American industries on the eve of the Civil War. As Table 2-6 shows, the first five industries in terms of value added by manufacturing were cotton goods, lumbering, boots and shoes, flour and meal, and men's clothing. Industries fabricating iron and manufacturing machinery account for less than 10 percent of the total.

But this is not all. Valuable studies by Paul A. David emphasize the relatively greater possibility in America of making a *joint* substitution of natural resources and capital for scarce labor. For example, supplies of wood in the United States were far more abundant and cheap than in England, whose timber supplies had been depleted by centuries of use for shipbuilding, iron smelting, and construction. This made it possible for some of America's capital equipment to be constructed of wood, for example, early textile machinery. Methods of production that were capital-intensive could thus be employed, and since innovation occurs at the capital-intensive end of the spectrum of production methods, one can say that the relative resource abundance in America encouraged more innovation than would have been the case had a larger quantity of labor per unit of output been used.

Table 2-6
Output of Ten Leading Industries, 1859

Industry	Value added (millions of dollars)
1. Cotton goods	$54.7
2. Lumbering	53.6
3. Boot and shoe	49.2
4. Flour and meal	40.1
5. Men's clothing	36.7
6. Iron fabrication	35.7
7. Machinery	32.6
8. Woolen goods	25.0
9. Wagons	23.7
10. Leather	22.8

SOURCE: Secretary of the Interior, *The Eighth Census: Manufactures of the United States in 1860* (Washington, D.C.: Government Printing Office, 1865), pp. 733–42.

In addition, there is reason to believe that the United States had still another comparative advantage over the English. In a number of lines of production, the type of capital equipment employed required the input of raw materials (or land) that existed in the United States more abundantly and hence more cheaply than in England. Contemporary observers generally agreed, Edward Ames and Nathan Rosenberg point out, that the technological differences between England and the United States were most remarkable in the case of woodworking machinery. Popular in America, but neglected in England, these machines, made of metal, were not only laborsaving but also wasteful of wood. The example of the cotton textile industry may also be cited. That industry in England was dominated by the use of mule-spinning equipment, its American counterpart by ring-spinning machinery. Lars Sandberg has shown that the American machinery was not only more capital-intensive than the English, but also—and this is especially true for yarn counts above forty—that it required the use of more long-staple cotton, which was cheaper for Americans than for the English, per pound of yarn. Finally, Paul David himself has shown that "the efficient use of mechanical reapers required a level, stone-free farm terrain, arranged in large and regularly shaped enclosures—a specific natural resource input that at the midpoint of the nineteenth century was obtained much more cheaply (relative to the price of grain) in the United States than in the British Isles."

However, all of the story of the rise of manufacturing in the United States cannot be told in terms of the relative cheapness of domestic raw materials. Americans also learned how to organize and manage production in such a way as to save both capital and labor. They did so by adopting the factory system.

Underlying the rise of the factory system were two technical processes essential to mass production— manufacture by the method of interchangeable parts and the use of assembly-line techniques. Both procedures were practiced on a small scale early in our history. The independent contributions made to interchangeable parts manufacturing by Eli Whitney and Simeon North are well known, as is the assistance given Whitney by government contracts in the small-arms industry, to which field he first applied the method in the 1790s. Before the Civil War the technique was being used for the manufacture of firearms, clocks and watches, agricultural implements, and sewing machines. The beginnings of the assembly line date from Oliver Evans's introduction of the principle of a continuous process of production in a flour mill which he built in 1782. The importance of labor scarcity in inducing the principle is clearly to be seen in Evans's statement that it was he who "first conceived the grand design of applying the power that drives the millstones to perform all the operations which were hitherto effected by manual labor." His object, he added, was to "make the mill exceed all others." By the 1850s, Cyrus McCormick seems to have been employing both techniques in his Chicago reaper factory.

As we saw in Chapter I, large factories—those with assets of $100,000 or more, or with 250 or more workers—were overwhelmingly concentrated in the textile industry in the 1830s. The machines in these factories were mainly wooden and driven by water power, the latter beginning to be transmitted to the machines by leather belting. And for the most part children and young women made up the work force. After 1840 this scene changed dramatically. The factory quickly appeared in a number of other industries; for example, iron, iron working, glass, paper, and industries involving refining and distilling processes. In these industries the factory became increasingly powered by steam; used metal machinery; was manned by heads of families (i.e., by male labor, as distinguished from the women and children employed in the textile industry); and was located in the larger cities, rather than in rural areas adjacent to water-power sites. This more widespread substitution of machines for manual methods of production contributed to economic growth by increasing the productivity of labor. Not only labor was saved but capital as well, for metal machines could be run faster and longer than wooden ones, thus increasing output per unit of capital.

The diffusion of the factory system appears to have owed a great deal to a cheapening of the cost of fuel following the opening up of the anthracite coal fields in Pennsylvania in the early 1830s. Cheap anthracite replaced expensive charcoal and wood in the production and refining of wrought iron, reduced the price of iron, and encouraged large-scale manufacturing of iron products. At the same time, anthracite provided an inexpensive fuel for steam engines. While most steam engines continued to burn wood until 1860, the use of anthracite expanded in the late 1830s and 1840s. The result was that in the 1840s the manufacture of such tools as hoes, axes, rakes, and hammers; of such transportation equipment as railway wheels and locomotives; and of such agricultural equipment as harvesters, reapers, and plows, moved with a rush from small shops or mills to factories. John Deere's plows, it should be noted, had chilled steel moldboards, and the cutter bar of Cyrus McCormick and Obed Hussey's machines also used steel rather than iron.

The rise of these large metalworking enterprises led, in turn, to the beginnings of an industry that specialized in making machines for other industries—the machine tool industry. The more manufacturers mechanized, the wider the market for the machine-making industry. In the early part of the century, makers of machines did not exist as a separate industry. Manufacturers of various end-products mainly made their own machines. With increased mechanization, machine-making shops emerged as adjuncts to end-product factories, appearing first in the New England textile industry. These shops also made their own lathes, planers, and other machine tools, although some tools were imported from England. As the market for machines widened, a machine shop often undertook to produce several different types of machines, but after 1840 there occurred a high degree of specialization in their manufacture. According to Jonathan T. Lincoln, "With the wide extension of the railroads, locomotive-building became an important industry, too big to share quarters with spinning-frames and looms; and gradually the skill acquired in the building of machinery for the early factories was passed on and permeated the manufacture of machinery for many industries, in shops established for these specific purposes." By the 1850s visiting English technicians could observe that "in the adaptation of special apparatus to a single operation in almost all branches of industry, the Ameri-

cans display an amount of ingenuity, combined wi'h un-
daunted energy, which as a nation we should do well to
imitate." Particularly in woodworking and small arms,
Americans had developed machine tools more specialized
than those available in England. The 1850s and 1860s
witnessed the rapid rise of firms making highly specialized
machine tools.

There thus emerged during the forty years before the
Civil War an important capital goods sector of the economy
which increasingly specialized in the production of producers' durables—machines and machine tools. This new
sector not only responded to increasing demand for its
products by becoming more and more specialized. It had
every incentive to widen its market by adopting laborsaving improvements in manufacturing techniques which
would enable it to provide machines as cheaply as possible.
In consequence, the durable goods industry itself became a
main source of technological innovation that eventually
permitted capital saving for the economy as a whole.
Futhermore, the machine shops became important training schools for numerous machinists. Especially important
was the independent machine shop opened in 1810 in
Pawtucket, R. I., by David Wilkinson, a brother-in-law of
Samuel Slater. According to Lincoln, all the textile-
machine companies founded in the first half of the
nineteenth century, with one or two notable exceptions,
owed their origins to the skill imparted by Wilkinson.

The insight of a leading student of the history of
American technology, Nathan Rosenberg, enables us to
see that the acquisition and diffusion of specialized technical knowledge, a process of vital importance to an indus-

trializing economy, owed much to a phenomenon which he usefully describes as one of "technological convergence." The technical processes involved in the manufacture of machinery were common to many industries rather than unique within each of them. What gave these processes their common character was the basic fact that industrialization in the nineteenth century involved the growing adoption of a metal-using technology employing decentralized sources of power:

> The use of machinery in the cutting of metal into precise shapes involves, to begin with, a relatively small number of operations (and therefore machine types): turning, boring, drilling, milling, planing, grinding, polishing, etc. Moreover, all machines performing such operations confront a similar collection of technical problems, dealing with such matters as power transmission (gearing, belting, shafting), control devices, feed mechanisms, friction reduction, and a broad array of problems connected with the properties of metals (such as ability to withstand stresses and heat resistance). It is because these processes and problems became common to the production of a wide range of disparate commodities that industries which were apparently unrelated from the point of view of the nature and uses of the final product became very closely related (technologically convergent) on a technological basis—for example, firearms, sewing machines, and bicycles.

This emphasis on the machine tool industry as a key transmission center for expertise in the making and use of machinery, and upon the diffusion of knowledge as a prerequisite of industrialization, adds significantly to our understanding of the basic forces at work in that process.

Finally, we must note the contribution to growth made by management. According to Alfred D. Chandler, Jr., the subdivision of labor under the factory system— that is, the allocation of specialized skills to the performance of subdivided tasks—gave rise to a new class of professional business managers. In only a relatively few areas, such as the army and navy, and on southern plantations, had men been hired full time to direct the work of others. In the shops, mills, small mines, and transportation companies characteristic of the economy in 1830, the owners were managers. Working closely with their small laboring force, they themselves recruited, trained, and supervised workers, and assigned them their daily tasks. They also kept the simplest of accounting records. The coming of the factory system put an end to personal management. Size and subdivision raised new problems of coordinating and planning the work of many men, and of accounting for capital funds as well as working capital for materials and wages. The 1840s and 1850s, then, saw the beginnings of systematic organization and cost accounting in American industry. These years mark the genesis of modern management in America, the beginnings of productivity-enhancing activity in the business sector of manufacturing enterprise.

By 1860 both of the main commodity-producing sectors of the economy, agriculture and manufacturing, had taken significant early steps on the road to modernization. Both were in the process of increasing their use of the technological innovations embodied in new tools and equipment, and both were contributing to the growth of the economy by increasing the productivity of labor. But there was a key difference between the two sectors in this regard. In agriculture, machines enabled farmers to till more land, and had the nation not possessed this factor of production in rich abundance, increases in output per farmer would have been subject to diminishing returns more quickly. In a word, it was land-and-resource-using techniques of production that sustained the productivity gains of agriculture. In manufacturing, just the opposite was the case; and on the eve of the Civil War the factory system and early modern managerial practices were extending more widely processes of control of both labor and material resources, of more economical use, of the factors of production.

We turn now to the much-debated question of the effects of the Civil War on the process of industrialization.

THREE

The Civil War and the Postwar Industrial Revolution, 1861–1914

Not so many years ago historians looked upon the Civil War as a great divide separating modern America from its preindustrial past. To Charles and Mary Beard, for example, the war was a "second American Revolution" which ended in "the unquestioned establishment of a new power in the government, making vast changes in the arrangement of classes, in the accumulation and distribution of wealth, in the course of industrial development, and in the Constitution inherited from the Fathers." It seemed reasonable to believe that the federal government's contracts for guns, munitions, army uniforms, and other supplies must have created a massive set of demands which, given the particularly acute shortage of labor in wartime, could not have been filled without a widespread mechanization of industry. It seemed self-evident that with the political power of the agrarian South gone from the Union nothing could block the enactment of legislation favorable to northern industrial interests. Citing issuance of greenbacks, tariff increases, founding of the National Banking System, adoption of the Homestead Act, grants of land and other subsidies to the transcontinental railroads, passage of the Morrill Land Grant College Act, and adoption of contract labor laws, historians argued that federal legislation, together with wartime demand, accelerated the process of industrialization and paved the way for postwar growth in national income.

The argument is a plausible one. But is it true? And how shall we assess its validity? The logical requirements for testing it are clear enough. The essence of the argument lies in the belief that the Civil War made a difference, that it accelerated the rate of industrialization and growth of national income, that prewar rates of change in these phenomena were slower than postwar rates. We can therefore ask whether available statistical data support these claims. And since war-generated demands and federal legislation are made responsible for accelerated growth, we can also inquire into the growth record of the Civil War decade itself. Our inquiry, let us make clear in advance, will not turn out very favorably for the argument under assessment. Yet it must be acknowledged that questions remain for future research. One obvious source of residual uncertainty is the fact that we are still unable to make inferences about the behavior of total output during the years 1861–65. Discussions of the Civil War decade rest upon comparisons made between census years 1860 and 1870. We are, however, able to talk about the wartime output of particular industries.

Let us turn first to the question whether accelerated growth took place during the decade in which the war was fought. The answer is sharply negative. According to the estimates of Robert Gallman, increases in commodity output averaged only 2.0 percent per year between 1860 and 1870, the lowest growth rate of any decade in the nineteenth century. If we look at particular industries the story is much the same: output continued to grow during the war years, but at declining rates. Annual production of pig iron increased 24 percent from 1850 to 1855, 17 percent from 1855 to 1860, 1 percent from 1860 to 1865, and 100 percent from 1865 to 1870. The number of bales of cotton consumed in United States manufacturing rose 143 percent from 1840 to 1850 and 47 percent from 1850 to 1860, only to fall by 6 percent from 1860 to 1870. New railroad track laid from 1851 through 1855 totaled 11,627 miles, from 1856 to 1860 only 8,721 miles, and from 1861 through 1865, only 4,076 miles. While we do not know the rate of increase of output as a whole during the war years, the ground would appear firm for the presumption that the war had a retardative effect upon that rate.

We obtain results of a different kind when we compare prewar and postwar rates of growth in output per capita. In contrast with an annual rate of only 1.45 percent between 1840 and 1860, the rate measured 2.1 percent between 1870 and 1900. Does this mean that the Civil War accelerated the rate of growth in the later years of the postwar period? Not necessarily; indeed, probably not. As Stanley L. Engerman has suggested, the higher postwar rate "may merely reflect a 'catching-up' process induced by the decline in per capita commodity output during the Civil War decade." The possibility, he adds, is suggested by the fact that the immediate postwar years show the highest growth rate, and by the fact that the growth rate of per capita commodity output is the same between 1860 and 1900 and between 1840 and 1860.

Suppose we now take the opposite tack and suggest that the "true" explanation of the higher postwar rate of growth in per capita output is the rising share of manufacturing in output. Unhappily for that suggestion, Gallman's estimates indicate that the relative contribution made by manufacturing was larger before the war than afterwards. This follows from two considerations: (1) while the increase in the share of manufacturing in commodity output was equally as large—not larger—in the twenty years before the war as in the twenty years after it, (2) commodity output itself increased at a greater annual rate before the war (4.6% between 1840–60) than afterwards (4.4% between 1870 and 1900). If we shift the focus to value added in manufacturing, the conclusion is only reinforced: growth between 1840–60 proceeded at an annual rate of 7.8 percent, in contrast with 6 percent between 1870 and 1900. The results are even more devastating if we look at the decade of the Civil War itself. Between 1860 and 1870 value added by manufacturing increased at an annual rate of 2.3 percent, the lowest rate of increase of any decade in the nineteenth century; the manufacturing share in commodity output rose only from 32 percent to 33 percent; and labor productivity in manufacturing *fell* by 13 percent, a unique occurrence for the nineteenth century.

In sum, Engerman is probably correct in his suggestion that the higher postwar rate of growth in output per capita represents a "catching-up" phenomenon. He offers the same explanation for the fact that the share of capital goods in commodity output rose in the decade of the Civil War, reaching a nineteenth-century peak in 1870. Once again, he is probably right in suggesting that the rise is best understood in the light of probable declines in the earlier years of the decade. For the rate of growth of the stock of fixed capital fell from 8.5 percent in the 1850s to 4.1 percent in the 1860s. Finally, the stock of fixed capital in manufacturing grew more rapidly in the postwar years, at an annual rate of 6.8 percent, in comparison with a prewar rate of 6.3 percent. Had earlier historians known of this statistical finding they would undoubtedly have maintained that the higher postwar rate rested upon the shift toward mechanization they presumed to have occurred during the Civil War. As we have just seen, however, the chances are that the increased rate of growth in the capital stock came after the war. And there are additional good reasons for believing so.

By twentieth-century standards the Civil War was premodern. It was unmechanized and fought by men on foot or horseback armed with rifles, bayonets, and sabers. The consumption of iron attributable to small-arms production amounted merely to 1 percent of the total output of iron between 1861 and 1865. While artillery was used, it too was a minor consumer of iron and steel. The effect of the war on the agricultural implement industry is an unsettled question, however. One available set of figures shows increases in production of farm machinery of 110 percent from 1850 to 1860, 140 percent from 1860 to 1870, and 95 percent from 1870 to 1880. But the biographer of Cyrus McCormick, commenting on a survey of agricultural equipment manufactureres made in 1864, observes that "it is significant that very few of them increased their annual output since 1861." Moreover, production figures need to be offset by unavailable statistics on wartime destruction of agricultural machinery and set in the context of a rise in the number of farms by about one-third during the decade of the 1860s. The latter helps explain why the average value of machinery per farm *fell* nearly 25 percent in the decade of the war. More research is needed, however, because of the possibility that the machinery was concentrated on farms of larger size; that is, larger agricultural units may have undergone an increase in capital-intensive modes of production. In fine, wartime labor scarcity may have had a greater effect in agriculture than in manufacturing on the rate of growth in output per capita.

Since the available estimates of output growth do not support the contention that the Civil War exerted the positive effects in which earlier historians believed, it is hardly worthwhile to examine closely the relationship they thought they saw between federal legislation and subsequent acceleration. It is, however, decidedly worthwhile to point out in general terms the dangers in exercising in a casual way one's historical imagination. Historians have often displayed a fondness for suggesting the existence of relationships which seem to them plausible, but are too complex for detailed unraveling. Thus, on the face of it, it appeared reasonable that in some way or other cheaper land or free land (the Homestead Act), cheaper money (issuance of greenbacks), cheaper labor (contract labor laws), cheaper transport costs (grants of subsidies to transcontinental railroads), and diminished foreign competition (protective tariffs) should have encouraged manufacturing and income growth. The unexamined assumption behind casual suggestions of these kinds is that it is generally true that reductions in one or more of the costs of production (cause) are followed by accelerated growth (effect).

This may be. But we need to know a good deal more if we are to be able to judge the validity of the generalizations. Under what conditions are they valid? Under what conditions, for example, is a reduction in the cost of labor associated with an increase in output? Once we specify these conditions, we need to ask whether the apparent relationship is truly causal, or merely accidental. This we can determine only by examining other instances—as many as possible—in which, under similar conditions, the relationship is found to exist. Quests of this kind are essential to establish the frequency with which the two variables (decreased labor cost—increased output) are to be found in association. If the association is sufficiently regular to suggest the probability that the variables are related as cause and effect, if we are entitled to express the relationship in the form of a guarded generalization —that is, one whose operative value is limited to specified conditions of which we have a number of examples (although far fewer than would be obtainable if our problem were one of natural science rather than social science)— we may then confront the problem of explanation.

We explain a relationship by answering the question "why." And our answer must be logically mandated. "Given conditions a, b, c, why *should* a reduction in labor cost be followed by an increase in output?" Our answer must be logically mandated in the sense that it is deducible from a higher-level generalization, one whose operative range is broader, indeed, sufficiently broad so as to include our more narrow-range generalization as a particular case. It might take the form of some such statement as this: "Other things being equal, if unit production costs are reduced, ensuing reductions in price will be followed by increases in the quantity demanded and in output." And this is not the end of the matter. This higher-level generalization—"higher" because more abstracted from restrictive particulars and hence explanatory of a wider range of cases—must itself be deducible from a still higher-level generalization, for example, that "other conditions being equal,* economic enterprises tend to maximize their profits"—and this, in turn, perhaps, from a generalization concerning the behavior of rational beings.

This structure of ascending and more widely embracive generalizations is what is known as a "theory" or "model." All explanation requires theory. And since the days of Aristotle, the most prestigious form of explanation has been deductive in form. In sum, causal explanation involves two steps: (1) verification of the existence of a

---

*"Other conditions being equal" here refers to data given—that is, assumptions about such conditions as the existence of competitive markets, about elasticities of demand, etc. One must be careful always to specify the conditions in which the generalization holds.

dependably regular association between two or more variables, and (2) explanation of this relationship by deducing it from a generalization of wider scope, at a higher level of what may be usefully visualized as an inverted pyramid.

Historians are generally consumers rather than producers of theories and this is as it should be. Yet, ideally, they should be conscious of the theoretical implications of the relationships they think they see. At a minimum, they should ask whether the relationship is accidental rather than causal. No such efforts appear to have attended the suggestions we have cited. The fact is that economic growth and the acceleration of manufacturing enterprise went on during periods of low tariffs as well as high ones; in time of monetary stringency and monetary plenty; under land disposal policies of many kinds; and in the face of generally high labor costs. These things are true for the antebellum period and for the postwar period as well. As far as the tariff is concerned, a demonstration of its effects would appear to require something more than economic expertise. The impact of the tariff upon a single industry, let alone the entire economy, is still unknown. And that the development of industry did not require a prior development of railroads is conclusively shown by the growth of textile manufacturing in New England before the beginning of the railroad era in the 1830s. This is not to say that railroads did not encourage the further growth of manufacturing. The industrialization that occurred after the war may have been particularly dependent upon cheap or inland transportation. But the point remains: the totality of conditions in which railroads exerted this effect must be specified with care.

There is one additional argument that should be considered—that a redistribution of income via the government debt encouraged postwar growth. This argument holds that interest and principal on the debt were paid by regressive taxes after the war, that money was thus transferred from consumers to savers, and that this shift, by increasing the amount available for investment, encouraged the expansion of manufacturing. However, Stanley Engerman has made short shrift of the argument by inquiring into the magnitude of the effect of the shift. His conclusion is that the increase in the growth rate resulting from the additional capital formation would have been "about .09 of one percentage point—an amount less than one-fortieth of the observed growth rate of the period" from 1866 to 1890. Had the magnitude been larger than this, the question of the allocation of the additional capital between manufactures and other investment outlets would still have to be faced.

In sum, the available evidence suggests strongly that the Civil War inhibited America's economic growth. We are left to wonder why an opposing point of view remained unchallenged for so long. The answer may simply be that potential countervailing evidence was not marshaled before Gallman's work. Yet one suspects the presence of a contributing factor. The older view of the effects of the Civil War has an interesting pedigree. In the later years of the nineteenth century the belief was widely shared that the war had unlocked the energies of the nation for a glorious period of national growth. One finds this view expressed in late nineteenth century memoirs, for example, those of Grenville M. Dodge, chief engineer in charge of the construction of the Union Pacific Railroad, and those of the eminent lawyer Ralph D. Ingersoll, as well as in the writings of Mark Twain. As the latter put it, America "had just completed its youth, its ennobling WAR—strong, pure, clean, ambitious, impressionable —[and was] ready to make choice of a life-course and move with a rush." That historians should have perpetuated the myth is not surprising. As Thomas C. Cochran has suggested, given the great cost and human losses of the war, it was natural for Americans, who like to see their history in terms of optimism and progress, to believe that the war had the beneficent effects of achieving both freedom for blacks and industrial progress.

Industrial progress there was indeed. But it cannot be attributed to war.

In history no brief period of time is wholly dissimilar from its immediate past. To designate the years between the end of the Civil War and the early years of the twentieth century as the era of the American Industrial Revolution implies a discounting of the importance of the industrial thrust of 1840–60, as well as the industrial beginnings of still earlier years. It subtly downplays the urban and labor force growth and transport improvements that invigorated the antebellum economy. These things we do not intend. The developments that followed the war would be inconceivable without those which preceded it. Yet there are crucial differences between them, and the term "Industrial Revolution" usefully accentuates their significance. Above all, it was during these years following the Civil War that the nation laid the physical basis of a modern economy and learned how to organize the flow of its resources by techniques of modern management.

To lay the physical basis of a modern economy implies a process known as "capital deepening" a process in which savers and investors withhold from consumption a markedly increased share of the gross national product. All during these years, indeed from 1840 to 1900, the average annual rate of increase in the size of the capital stock (5.40%) much exceeded increases in the size of the labor force (2.77%) and the supply of land (2.93%). To be sure, even before the Civil War a substantial portion of GNP—from 14 percent to 16 percent—had been devoted to capital formation. Yet the postwar shares were higher in every decade than those before the war. By the 1870s the share amounted to 24 percent, and by the 1880s to 28 percent. In sum, the contribution of capital to growth during these years was not only relatively more important than the contribution of land and labor, in addition, a marked long-term rise in investment took place. Although, according to Robert Gallman, the timing and duration of the increase cannot be established precisely, we can say with assurance that the relevant time period extends between the decades 1834–43 and 1899–1908.

What were the leading sources of demand behind this quantum jump in capital formation? And how are the increases in supply to be explained? In the main, it was the process of industrialization—broadly but legitimately defined to include not only factories and their equipment, but also transportation and nonfarm construction, especially urban housing—that generated the increases in demand. In the thirty years between 1870–1900 industry continued its relative rise and agriculture its relative decline, the former increasing from 43 percent to 65 percent, the latter falling from 57 percent to 35 percent, of value added by these two sectors of the economy. Between 1870 and 1890 alone the nation added 114,000 miles of track to its railroad system. The growth of population, labor force, and urban centers also increased the demand for capital. Between 1870 and 1900 population rose from 40 million to 76 million, and the labor force from about 13 million to 29 million. The urban percentage of the population increased from roughly 26 percent to 40 percent. With more people and workers, there was every inducement to accumulate more capital to supply workers with tools, households with residences, businesses with buildings, and society as a whole with more roads, bridges, railroads, hospitals, schools, and inventories.

Clearly, it is during this period that we can first speak of the mass demand of a national urban market—a market created by the railroads and sustained in effectiveness by rising per capita incomes. The latter had averaged only a 1.45 percent increase per year between 1840–60; between 1870–1900 the rate rose to 2.1 percent. More broadly, Paul A. David and Moses Abramovitz have found that "between the first and second halves of the century the long-term per capita output growth rate accelerated, increasing by roughly 0.5 percentage points to the 1.7–1.9 percent level per annum which has been maintained in the United States economy throughout the last one hundred years." Thus, the period witnessed a

quantum leap in the scale of demand for goods and services. Had the supply response to this demand been
inadequate, rising levels of material well-being would
have been checked. Mass demand therefore called for
mass production.

Mass production held out the promise of economies
of scale or reduced costs per unit of output over a wide
range of output. To achieve production in high volume,
however, required enlarged plant and equipment. The
latter, in turn, required not only technological feasibility,
but adequacy of finance: not only must the nation's stock
of knowledge—and not least its administrative skills—
respond to the demands of more technical tasks, but capital markets must also respond. These responses, as we shall
see, were indeed forthcoming, and in the ensuing discussion we shall emphasize particularly the institutional
changes that made the responses possible. It is reasonable
to believe that these institutional changes, together with
the economies of scale flowing from the production of
manufactured goods in large volume, generated most of
the productivity gains realized during the period.

The sources of demand for capital in the rapidly
industrializing economy could not be more clear. The
sources of supply are more difficult to explain. Capital
formation must be financed, and finance requires savings.
Did the rate of savings go up? The answer given this
question by Lance E. Davis, a leading student of the
subject, is affirmative. According to Davis, a substantial
increase in the savings/income ratio took place between
the decades 1830–80. The essential problem is to explain
the sources of the increase.

Foreign accumulations invested in the United States are less troublesome to explain than their domestic counterparts. Surpluses of capital existed in the maturer economies of Europe, and returns were less attractive there than in areas of capital deficit. In consequence, net capital flows amounting to $1.5 billion entered the developing American economy between 1830 and 1880, and an additional $2 billion entered between 1870 and 1895. Most of the investment went into municipal and other local bonds, and into railroads and public utilities, although a few manufacturing firms were also among the recipients. English investors were the primary source of the flow.

Unfortunately, estimates of the volume of domestic savings by governments, businesses, and households begin only with the year 1898. Even so, there is no reason to doubt that domestic savings far outstripped foreign investment before then. It is also undoubtedly true that household or "personal" savings were far more important than any other domestic source. Why, then, did personal savings rise?

The question is a difficult one both because of the number of forces that may have contributed to this result and because of the paucity of our information about them. Among the many factors upon which savings depend are the level of income; the degree of inequality in its distribution (the greater that inequality the larger the savings, since it is receivers of large incomes who do most of the saving); and a variety of conditions affecting the utility of savings—including interest rates, the price level, tastes and living standards, and the effects of technological change upon available goods and services. The net impact of these and other influences at play during the middle and later decades of the nineteenth century cannot be sifted with assurance.

In Davis's judgment, most of the increase in the savings/income ratio came from the development of a set of financial institutions, the function of which was to mediate between saving and investment. These financial intermediaries—commercial banks, savings banks, and life insurance companies—both increased the options of savers and improved the process by which savings were mobilized and made available to investors. However, other institutions also played an important part in the development of markets for long-term capital. Of these, we may single out the New York Stock Exchange and, above all, the corporation itself. All of these institutions had been in existence before the Civil War, but with the great leap in the demand for finance they expanded in numbers, volume of business, and functions. Growth did not proceed with equal rapidity in all sections of the country—the postwar South, especially, lagged behind—but by the time of World War I a truly national capital market had evolved, supplementing concentrations of capital that were merely local or regional. A thumbnail sketch of the rise of these institutions will clarify the increasingly important part they came to play in the processes of saving and capital formation. In their absence, the capital deepening that marks the era of the Industrial Revolution could not have occurred.

Commercial banks were unknown in the colonial period of American history. This does not mean that money and credit did not then exist. On the contrary, colonial governments issued paper money (bills of credit) from time to time, and British exporters extended long credits of a year or more to colonial importers. The latter, in turn, sold on credit to urban and rural storekeepers. The commercial paper arising from these transactions —bills of exchange and promissory notes (i.o.u.'s)— helped augment scarce supplies of specie (gold or silver coins) by serving along with bills of credit as means of payment. The advent of the Revolution cut off the credit upon which the trade of the colonies had depended and at the same time undermined the paper money issued by colonial governments. When the new states under the Constitution relinquished the right to emit bills of credit, the need for the facilities of commercial banks became imperative.

The subsequent growth of commercial banks was rapid. Merely three in number in 1789, there were more than 200 in 1815, 700 in 1835, 1,300 in 1855, and 1,500 in 1860. The overwhelming majority of these institutions received their charters of incorporation from the states, and in the earlier years of the century, although not only then, a special law was enacted to bring each of them into existence. Most northern and western states, however, passed "free" (i.e., general) banking legislation during and after the 1830s and this made state charters easier to obtain. Passage of the National Bank Act in 1863 opened an alternative route to charter even in states with restrictive banking laws. Thus facilitated, the number of banks more than doubled between 1860 and 1880, and by 1900 their number exceeded 12,000.

Commercial banks contributed in three ways to the process of saving. In the first place, like other corporations they raised capital by selling their stocks and bonds. Thus their securities encouraged saving by providing an outlet for it. In the second place, commercial banks also served as depositories for savings. Had the banks transferred these savings dollar for dollar to investors they would have facilitated the mobilization of capital. They did far more than this, however. Unlike savings banks, which could transfer only the money they received, commercial banks also created money.

They did so by establishing a credit against which borrowers might draw by check and, before 1865, also by making loans in the form of banknotes. When they established a credit, what they did in essence was to create a deposit; its effect was just as though a customer had lodged money in the bank for safekeeping. Whatever the form of the loan, however—whether created deposits or banknotes—the volume of loans usually exceeded by three or more times the amount of specie kept in reserve. Experience taught bankers that some but not all of their customers might wish to have their banknotes converted into specie or their checks cashed in that form. Since banknotes were essentially i.o.u.'s—promises made by the issuing bank to pay specie to bearer on demand— reserves had to be kept, but as a rule they might safely be fractional reserves, rather than reserves matching outstanding loans dollar for dollar. State banknotes ceased to be an element of the circulating currency after 1865, but commercial bankers still had to maintain fractional monetary reserves against their loans and other liabilities.

The volume of commercial bank credit expanded considerably in the second half of the nineteenth century. Banknotes and deposits together fell short of a half billion dollars in 1860, but by 1900 deposits alone amounted to nearly $7 billion. As a rule this credit was limited to short periods, but frequent renewals often converted it into long-term loans that helped finance agriculture and transport development, as well as merchant inventories and industrialization. Commercial bank credit thus played an important role in a country undergoing development with scarce supplies of capital. In a fundamental sense, that credit represented saving not yet realized, but anticipated.

A third kind of saving contributed to by commercial banks was involuntary in nature. As we have just seen, banks increased the money supply by making loans to the business community (i.e. producers). Whenever the economy's resources were fully employed, though, the effect of such loans was to raise the price level (i.e., reduce the value of the dollar). Unlike producers, consumers had the same number of dollars as before, but because they were worth less they commanded a smaller share of income. Inflation thus effected a redistribution of income from consumers to producers, increasing the volume of involuntary saving. Since the course of the general price level was a downward one between 1869 and 1896, involuntary saving was a local or regional phenomenon, rather than a national one, during these years.

Savings banks made a lesser but still important contribution to the process of capital accumulation. Originating in the early nineteenth-century as philanthropic institutions designed to encourage thrift in the poor, they soon spread rapidly in the northern and Middle Atlantic states. Their number increased from 10 in 1820, to 61 in 1840, and to 278 in 1860; at the same dates total depositors rose, in round numbers, from 9,000, to 79,000, and to 694,000—while deposits themselves increased from $1 million, to $14 million, and to $149 million. By 1880, well over 2 million depositors had placed $819 million in savings banks: by 1900 depositors exceeded 6 million and deposits fell just short of $2.5 billion.

It is the uses to which these deposits were put that make the savings banks relevant to capital formation. In the first place, many of the savings banks came to be capital suppliers to commercial banks, not only by redepositing their own deposits in those institutions but also by investing in their stock. Their trustees often formed interlocking directorates with the officials of commercial banks. In New England, many were virtually savings departments of the commercial banks. Mortgage loans were common, but many also made loans on the security of bank stock, or themselves invested in bank stock and in such other corporate securities as railroad and canal stock. In addition, some of them also made direct loans to transportation companies and to industrialists.

We may be equally brief in our discussion of the life insurance company, an institution which combines the functions of saving, insurance, and investment. Early marine and fire insurance companies had sometimes written life policies and annuities, but the first company to specialize in life insurance was not incorporated until 1812. Significant expansion came only with the development of reliable mortality tables in the 1840s. At the beginning of that decade, the amount of life insurance in force totaled less than $5 million; by 1860, the amount exceeded $170 million. As Lance Davis points out, rapid growth came with the innovation of tontine and industrial insurance contracts after 1870. In the final quarter of the century the resources of life insurance companies quadrupled, jumping from $403 million to $1.7 billion. By 1900, 84 companies had more than $7.5 billion of life insurance in force.

The contribution of these companies to the process of industrialization can be seen in the ways in which they invested their funds. Beginning in the early 1880s leading firms began to invest heavily in railroad bonds, and by 1904 these issues accounted for one-third of their total assets. Overall figures for direct industrial investment are unavailable, but the process itself may be illustrated by the case of the Massachusetts Hospital Life Insurance Company. Before 1830 this company concentrated its investments in farm mortgages in western Massachusetts. In the 1830s, securities and business loans became more important in its portfolio, and the locus shifted to the neighborhood of Boston and to the textile industry. In the 1840s the company played a singularly important role in the textile capital market as a source of long-term loans. By 1890, more than half of its loans went to textile companies in Massachusetts, New Hampshire, and Maine— companies whose combined capital represented more than one-fourth of the textile capital of those states.

Of the institutions other than financial intermediaries whose rise was indispensable to the process of capital mobilization—the transfer of accumulations from savers to those who wish to use them—none was more important than the corporation. Indeed, the financial intermediaries were themselves incorporated enterprises. The use of this form of business organization was essential if the large capital sums required for industrial and transport expansion were to be raised. For the corporation by its very nature was a device for pooling the savings of large numbers of small investors. Even so, it must not be assumed that the advent and spread of the device of incorporation automatically guaranteed the ability to mobilize large capital sums for use in manufacturing. Ease in mobilization also requires well-developed capital markets in which industrial shares can be bought and sold. While such markets were growing in the final quarter of the nineteenth century, it was not until the last five years of the century that the New York Stock Exchange listed a considerable number of industrials. The thinness of this and other capital markets before 1895 has special pertinence, as we shall see, to the initially high degrees of concentration achieved in a number of new growth industries. But let us first trace the early nature and uses of the corporation and outline the process by which it rose to prominence as a device not only for mobilizing capital, but also for managing the flow of resources in the manufacturing and transport sectors of the economy.

A group of individuals authorized by law to act as a unit, a fictitious legal person with its own name, in which it could sue and be sued, hold and transfer property, the corporation possessed distinct advantages over other forms of business enterprise. It is true that long before the existence of corporations, unchartered joint-stock companies, essentially large partnerships, had mobilized the large sums required in European mining and trade. But partnerships, no matter how great their size, came to an end with the death of a partner. Furthermore, in the event of bankruptcy, an individual partner stood to lose not only his investment but also his personal property— for the latter was subject to attachment to pay the debts of the partnership. From the beginning, the corporation possessed a longevity independent of those investing in it, and the gradual working out in the law of the principle of limited liability provided security against the latter risk.

Not surprisingly, in view of far more modest capital needs and accumulations, business corporations scarcely existed in the colonial period. Those that did—a water company in Boston and William Penn's Free Society of Traders in Pennsylvania in the seventeenth century; two groups of wharf proprietors, three water companies, and a mutual fire insurance company in the eighteenth century—were essentially instruments of public service. Perhaps more surprisingly, the objective of public service goes far to explain the formation of corporations in the early decades after independence. State governments created some 300 business corporations between the end of the Revolution and 1801, and the provision of inland navigation, turnpikes, and toll bridges was the purpose of two-thirds of them. Like the chartered joint-stock companies with which the English had pioneered in the settlement of America—the Massachusetts Bay Company

and the Virginia Company of London—early corporations were quasi-public agencies of the state. "Be it
enacted by the Senate and House of Representatives in
General Court assembled," reads a Massachusetts statute
of 1818, that the following named individuals "hereby are
constituted a corporation and *body politic*" for the purpose of erecting a flour mill. As bodies politic these corporations, like their predecessors, were accorded certain
exclusive privileges in order to encourage the devotion of
scarce private capital to public ends. Among these
privileges were monopoly rights of way, tax exemption,
the right of eminent domain, and the right, granted to
many nonbanking corporations, to facilitate the raising of
needed capital by engaging in banking operations and
conducting lotteries.

As capital accumulated, however, the line between
public interest and private advantage became more
sharply visible to critics of the privileges enjoyed by
corporations. Moreover, abuse easily crept into the
prevailing system of obtaining charters. Except for New
York and Connecticut, which in 1811 and 1817 respec-
tively passed general laws permitting qualified incorporators of certain kinds of manufacturing concerns to apply
to the secretary of state for a charter, incorporation by
special act of the state legislature was everywhere the
rule before the late 1830s. Lobbying expense, delay, and
bribery often accompanied efforts to obtain charters.
Men of agrarian temperament, who deplored the rapid
economic and social changes that were subordinating
older and simpler modes of life to urban business values,
complained—to cite the words of President Andrew

Jackson—of "the multitudes of corporations with exclusive privileges which they have succeeded in obtaining in different States." Those of an entrepreneurial persuasion resented specially privileged banking corporations in particular. As Jackson's secretary of the treasury, Roger B. Taney, once remarked: "There is perhaps no business which yields a profit so certain and liberal as the business of banking and exchange; and it is proper that it should be open, as far as practicable, to the most free competition and its advantages shared by all classes of society." Later, as Chief Justice of the Supreme Court, Taney was to strike a telling blow in favor of free, competitive enterprise by holding, in the *Charles River Bridge* case (1837), that a corporate charter could not confer implied powers beyond the specific terms of its grant. The decision freed new businesses from the fear of claims of monopoly on the part of older corporations with ambiguously phrased charters.

These various attacks on corporate privilege and enterprise restrictions had two important consequences. New York's passage of a free banking act in 1838 served as an important precedent for similar laws in other states. More than a half dozen states, moreover, passed general incorporation laws prior to the Civil War. But while an increasing number of charters were taken out under general laws, the lure of special advantages from special acts led most incorporators to prefer the older method until about 1875. The second important consequence was a tendency to seek charters of incorporation in expanding fields of enterprise. With widening use, the older view of the business corporation as an instrument of public service gave way still more to one emphasizing its utility for private profit.

A rapid increase in charters granted in the 1850s heralded the dawn of the age of the private business corporation. Yet it was only the dawn. Industrial techniques requiring large capital investment were of recent origin in important fields and made their way but slowly among constituent firms. Not until after 1835 did textile machinery become metal, large-scale, and expensive. Not until 1839 were the first successful coke-smelting furnaces built in the United States. As late as 1869 nearly half the mechanical power used in manufacturing was still derived directly from waterwheels and turbines rather than derived from steam engines. Lateness and lag had important consequences, for it is not so much the first appearance of new techniques as it is their spread that matters in economic growth. Imitation is just as important as innovation.

Among the significant causes of imitative lag must be set not only the inertia of traditional and less costly methods: Ignorance also counted for much, and what abetted it was the scarcity or lack of technical journals, trained engineers, and cost accounting techniques. The gradual overcoming of these obstacles contributed in the post-Civil War years to a wider dissemination of mechanized production methods. But on the eve of that conflict it was not corporations but individual proprietorships and partnerships that were able to amass the capital required for the control of most of the resources devoted to manufacturing.

The second half of the nineteenth century is marked

by three principal developments in the life of the private business corporation. There occurred, in the first place, a phenomenal expansion in the use of the corporate form, especially in such fields as iron and steel, nonferrous metals, textiles, chemicals, and liquor. Indeed, manufacturing corporations have constituted a large percentage of all charters granted each year since 1875. From the late 1870s until the mid-1890s incorporation proceeded at an extremely rapid rate, and by the end of the century two-thirds of the nation's industrial output was the product of incorporated enterprise. The second principal development of the half-century was a notable growth in size of the individual unit of enterprise. The dominance of the manufacturing sector by corporations, that is to say, was not ascribable to the increase in the number of charters alone. In a third development, there began to take place during the 1880s such remarkable changes in administrative organization as to justify the conclusion of the leading student of these developments, Alfred D. Chandler, Jr., that the decade saw the emergence of the modern corporation.

All of these changes had their origins in the widening markets that characterize the era. The first transcontinental railroad was completed in 1869, and between 1870 and 1914 railroad builders laid an astounding total of 200,000 miles of track, a growing proportion of it west of the Mississippi. The spreading railroad net helped settle the farmer's "last frontier," and during the half-century following the Civil War farmers occupied more land than in all the previous years of American history. At the same time, increasingly mechanized farms sent output soaring to new levels per capita and released unneeded farm workers to the rapidly expanding cities. The more the cities grew, in turn, the greater the demand for agricultural commodities and raw materials for urban and export markets. Urban growth also intensified the demand for the products of industries manufacturing consumer goods. Between 1880 and 1907 incorporation for the manufacture of food and kindred products, textile mill products, and other consumer goods bulked large among total incorporations. Indeed, the researches of Chandler show that it was the consumer goods industries that were first to become dominated by great business enterprises. By the beginning of the twentieth century, however, a swelling number of companies were engaged in the manufacture of machinery for the use of producers, rather than of goods for urban consumers or farmers.

In a number of industries—especially such new growth industries as petroleum, steel, milling, and meat packing—access to informal sources of finance played a crucial part in the early rise of individual firms to positions of dominance. Substantial sums had to be obtained if firms were to be able to adopt the capital-intensive technologies required by broadening national markets. A single comparison will reveal the wholly new dimensions of their task. Before the Civil War the largest manufacturers—the textile companies—needed less than a million dollars for their plant and equipment. In 1910, the net book value of Standard Oil exceeded $600 million! The problem was that the markets for industrial securities were insufficiently developed before the closing years of the century. As late as the 1880s an investor interested in purchasing industrial issues would have been more likely to turn to Boston than to the New York market, and even in Boston the market was very thin. In New York it was only in the late 1880s that it became possible to sell the preferred stock of manufacturing firms; and not until a decade later did the endorsement of J.P. Morgan, the enormously prestigious investment banker, make it possible to raise large sums through the sale of their common stock. Managers of industrial firms had no choice but to turn to other sources of finance, and in this effort some proved notably more successful than others.

In steel, it was Andrew Carnegie's talent in finance that enabled his firm to utilize the new Bessemer process in the 1870s. In meat packing in the 1880s and 1890s, the ability of Philip Armour, Gustavus Swift, and a few others to borrow from commercial banks, personal friends, and other sources enabled their firms to adopt the capital-intensive innovation of the refrigerator car. Loans from commercial banks in Cleveland enabled Rockefeller to utilize technical developments in oil refining conducive to substantial economies of scale. In these and other similar cases access to finance gave distinctive advantages to successful firms. Because of the amount of capital required and the difficulty in raising it, the entry of competitors was inhibited, and output became concentrated in a handful of large corporations. Further development of the capital markets, especially those following upon Morgan's reorganization of the railroad system in the 1880s, made it possible to finance the giant merger movement which swept over the manufacturing and mining sector of the economy in the late 1890s.

Size had distinct advantages. Besides the ability to turn out a substantial volume of goods at low unit costs, the large corporation could hire a more highly skilled management, market its goods more effectively, and finance itself more cheaply via profits retained in the business. There were also potential disadvantages. The large firm had to bear high overhead costs on its fixed capital investment in plant and machinery. Charges for depreciation, interest, and obsolescence eroded capital values and helped create a portentous situation, for railroads as well as manufacturers. In times of falling prices business managers tended to maintain production and compete vigorously for sales at any price rather than allow their heavily burdened plants to remain idle. Sales at low prices provided some income. Given a long period of falling prices this was a situation in which not only smaller firms, but also larger ones of lesser efficiency, could have little hope for survival.

The years from 1873 to 1896 constituted precisely such a period of long-term falling prices. In this setting the American business arena became a jungle in which many failed to survive bitterly competitive price cutting. With prices (and railroad rates) being driven to margins of cost and below, it became evident that one way to stay alive was to lower that margin by reducing costs. The achievement of greater efficiencies in production promised to do this. Larger firms therefore began during the 1880s to turn in increasing numbers to the sanctuary of vertical integration. They sought to reduce marketing and other costs by bringing under their control all the processes of production from raw materials to end product. In many cases, however, large firms also sought to assure themselves supplies of raw materials.

Competition among firms in the consumer goods industries resulted not only in *external* vertical integration, but also in a corresponding *internal* integration within individual firms. It was from this internal integration that the modern corporation emerged. To appreciate the nature of the changes in these industries it is necessary to realize that in the period prior to the rise of a national urban market individual firms generally relied upon commission agents for the procurement of their raw materials and for the sale of finished products in markets that were located more than a few miles from the factory. Vertical integration involved the abandonment of this system in favor of nationwide procurement and marketing organizations that were an integral part of the firm itself. In instances where the product had an element of newness and was particularly suited to the urban market, its makers first built up a large marketing apparatus in the form of branch houses, then followed this by creating a purchasing organization. Where the product was already an established one, large numbers of small manufacturers tended first to enter into a horizontal combination before proceeding to vertical integration. Whichever the sequence, a producing and distributing unit emerged which was not only larger in size but was also one in which operations were geographically dispersed. Their separation in space, and the individuality of their technical tasks, raised the problem of how best to conduct each separate operation and at the same time coordinate all of them to the optimum advantage of the firm as a whole.

The solution of the problem required not only clear distinctions between functions of field offices and headquarters, but also a careful allocation of responsibilities at headquarters as well.

The headquarters of business enterprises had been slow in developing. In the early nineteenth century the merchant in foreign trade had been the typical business figure. His headquarters was his countinghouse (office), and therein he supervised the routine tasks of a bookkeeper and a clerk or two, besides giving thought to investment opportunities by which his house might prosper. Needing no large force of permanent employees, he relied mainly on the services of commission agents. Early nineteenth-century industrial enterprises similarly purchased their raw materials and sold their finished goods by means of commission agents, although sometimes utilizing the selling services of wholesalers. Their headquarters, too, were small. Many large textile mills employing hundreds of workers were run with practically no office force at all. Before the Civil War, the railroads appear to have been the only enterprises to divide their headquarters into functional departments. The vertical integration movement, which competition in postwar national markets so accentuated, not only accelerated this process of departmentalization but also obliged businessmen to work out problems of coordination between headquarters and field. This the modern corporation proceeded to do by setting up a separate functional department for each major activity: production or purchasing of raw materials, manufacturing, marketing, and finance.

At the head of each department was placed a specialist in the activity for which that department was given responsibility. Normally a vice-president, and supreme in his own sphere, he was assigned a managing director to handle departmental routine. Each vice-president fulfilled two main duties. In the first place he had the responsibility for the broader developments of his department. In the second, he served as a member of an executive committee composed of all department heads, together with the president and the chairman of the board of directors. The executive committee, in turn, had three functions. It coordinated the various activities of the enterprise, both interdepartmentally at the headquarters level and also between headquarters and field, for the purpose of assuring a steady flow of product from raw materials to ultimate consumer. It made plans for the maintenance and expansion of the enterprise as a whole. And it appraised the performance of the entire organization.

In performing these functions, the executive committee came more and more to rely on accounting and statistical information in regard to costs, output, purchases, and sales. The large-scale operations of the modern corporation thus permitted specialization in the performance of various managerial functions, and specialization meant greater proficiency in each of them. Only from such specialization could there have emerged expert accounting techniques which permitted the substitution of scientific procedures for rule-of-thumb methods of operation. The work of Frederick W. Taylor in scientific management, which a number of modern corporations were soon to make use of in their continued drive for cost-reducing efficiencies, was a natural by-product of the trend toward specialization and cost accounting.

The modern corporation, appearing first in the consumer goods industries in the 1880s, transformed the leading firms therein by the early years of the twentieth century. Its first major appearance in industries making goods for producers dates from the 1890s. A highly structured mechanism, combining functional specialization with administrative centralization, it gave to firms adopting its procedures such competitive advantages as to compel adoption of those procedures by other leading firms in the same industry. Smaller companies, unable to compete except in small and specialized markets, tended to be absorbed or forced into bankruptcy. Competitive pressures in national markets thus served as an important factor in company growth, sometimes in conjunction with technological compulsions making for the same end, sometimes independently of them. The upshot was an even greater tendency for national markets to be dominated by a lessening number of large firms. Even greater, therefore, were the burdens of high overhead costs, the pressures to produce and sell, and the prospects of ruin for all from either uncontrolled production or competitive price wars. Only some form of combination held out any hope of salvation. "Combinations, syndicates, trusts—" Andrew Carnegie frankly admitted, "They are willing to try anything."

The first attempt at combination among producers usually took the form of a "gentleman's agreement." This was a verbal agreement to set and maintain prices, although it sometimes also included common policies regarding cash discounts and other trade practices. When the object of combination could not readily be agreed upon in an informal manner, business managers favored a written contractual agreement known as the "pool." Pools were formed for various purposes. In a "patent pool," the use of a new device or process was thereby confined to a restricted group. In a "profit pool," profits were paid into a central fund and then divided up on the basis of the percentage of total sales in a given period. Probably the main use of the pool was as a device to restrict output. This was effected by dividing the total market and assigning each producer a portion of it. Sometimes division was made on the basis of output, with each producer being assigned the sale of a given number of units; sometimes a territorial division was made, in which case each was assigned a designated sales area. While pools had not been unknown even before the Civil War, they were comparatively little used until after 1875. In the 1880s and 1890s they were to be found in such important industries as those making whiskey, salt, meat products, explosives, steel rails, structural steel, cast-iron pipe, and tobacco products. Comparable to the European cartel, the pool differed from its counterpart in this key respect: under the English common law, recognized in every state except Louisiana, the pool was regarded as an illegal, and hence unenforceable, restraint of trade.

Both gentlemen's agreements and pools may be said to have "worked," if only temporarily. Indeed, there can be no doubt that both forms of combination continue in use in the contemporary United States. But these relatively loose forms of collusion had serious disadvantages. For one thing, to the degree that they were successful in raising prices and achieving a monopoly profit, they encouraged new firms to enter the field. For another, although one of the main aims of collusion was the maintenance of prices during periods of deflation, it was precisely at such times that the temptation to violate agreements was strongest. A firm might exceed its assigned output or sell in forbidden territory, in which case other pool members had no legal way of compelling it to adhere to its agreement. Some more foolproof system was required and business managers found this in various "close-knit" arrangements.

The first and most famous of these was worked out in the depression-ridden 1870s by a man who was perhaps the shrewdest business manager of a generation of shrewd men. The man was John D. Rockefeller and the idea was the trust. The device of trusteeship is a very old one, but Rockefeller's Standard Oil Company put it to a new use. Employing ruthlessly competitive business practices, Rockefeller and his associates had succeeded during the 1870s in gaining control of more than 90 percent of the oil-refining capacity of the country. In 1882, they induced the stockholders of forty oil companies to turn their shares over to nine trustees. The trustees thus acquired voting control of the forty companies. In place of the stock, its former owners received "trust certificates" entitling them to dividends. So profitable did this device prove, and so successful as a means of centralizing control of an entire industry, that it was soon imitated. During the 1880s trusts were formed to control production in tobacco, sugar, whiskey, cotton seed oil, linseed oil, and lead industries.

The fatal defect of the trust form of combination was that the agreements were a matter of public record. Since in the eyes of the common law conspiracies in restraint of trade or attempts to monopolize were illegal, the prospects of longevity for trusts were not good once suits were brought against them in state courts. A number of suits were in fact begun in the 1880s, and in consequence of one of them, the Supreme Court of Ohio ordered Standard Oil to withdraw from the trust on the ground that it was attempting to create a monopoly. It was clear that some other form of combination would have to be used in place of the trust.

At this juncture the state of New Jersey in 1888 stepped into the breach and revised its general incorporation laws to allow corporations to purchase and hold the securities of one or more subsidiary corporations. Under these laws it proved relatively easy for the resulting "holding company" to bring a number of previously independent firms under unified control. The nonvoting preferred stockholders and bondholders need not even be consulted. Indeed, voting common stock was often so widely distributed that it was possible to exercise effective control by purchasing far less than 50 percent of it. New Jersey's Holding Company Act proved so successful in bolstering that state's finances with revenues from incorporation fees that other states soon liberalized their corporation laws in an effort to induce businesses to seek their charters from them.

Holding companies were to play a conspicuous role

in the great merger movement of 1895–1904. Producing nothing, selling nothing, they were incorporated solely to serve as an instrument of "consolidation" where the number of companies to be merged, or the size of their capital stocks, was large. The sale or exchange of shares in the holding company for a controlling number of shares in the companies to be merged permitted the consolidation to take place. At the same time, the fact that the New York Stock Exchange had developed to the point where the holding company's shares could be listed, and their rising prices noted by stockholders contemplating whether or not to exchange their shares for those of the holding company, increased the stockholders' willingness to make such an exchange. Promoters of mergers might use the technique of "acquisition," in which the sums required were sufficiently small as to be within the command of a firm already in existence. Thus, a clear commentary on the size of affected capital stocks is provided by the fact that holding companies figured in fully 86 percent of the mergers consummated in this period.

Mergers took place at the turn of the century in all major manufacturing and mining industries, but most were concentrated in primary metals, food products, petroleum products, chemicals, transportation equipment, fabricated metal products, machinery, and bituminous coal. Altogether a total of 319 consolidations occurred, with the period 1898–1902 representing peak years. The total capitalization involved was $6.3 billion, with 40 percent of that total being accounted for by only 29 percent of the 319 consolidations. Each of these larger consolidations involved had an authorized capitalization of

$50 million or more. One of them—U.S. Steel—had a capitalization of $1.37 billion—the first billion dollar corporation in history. (It alone accounted for 23% of the total capitalization.)

While the number of consolidations taking place affords us one view of the size of the merger wave, another is supplied by the number of firms disappearing into mergers. (When firms were consolidated by a holding company they continued to do business under their original firm names; firms acquired by a corporation already in existence lost their original names and "disappeared" into merger.) Disappearances averaged 301 a year between 1895–1904, but, as in the case of consolidations, the years 1898–1902 are of special prominence. In the year 1899 alone 1,028 firms disappeared into mergers.

The effect of the great turn-of-the-century merger wave on American industry was widespread and enduring. From it emerged U.S. Steel, American Tobacco, International Harvester, Du Pont, Corn Products, Anaconda Copper, and American Smelting and Refining —to name only a few of the giants of the twentieth century. Indeed, of the 100 largest corporations in the country in 1955, 20 were born during the period 1895–1904. According to one conservative estimate, by 1904, 318 firms had come into possession of 40 percent of all manufacturing assets. The absolute size of many of the new companies was not their only disturbing feature. Even more disturbing was their size in relation to the markets they served. As a result of the 1895–1904 merger wave a single firm came to account for 60 percent or more of total output in at least fifty different industries. Du

Pont, General Electric, Pullman, and American Tobacco were among sixteen companies controlling 85 percent or more of their respective markets. Surely the principal result, and probably also the principal purpose of the mergers—since most of the consolidations were horizontal in nature—was the control of price and output. Only in this way, it was believed, could cutthroat competition be brought to an end.

Yet it is important to keep in mind that the high degree of concentration implicit in these figures for market control has not increased in American industry since 1906. In fact, the degree of concentration may have somewhat lessened. While Supreme Court decisions under the Sherman Act (1890) may in part be responsible for this, Lance Davis emphasizes the contribution made by further development of the capital markets. By democratizing the sources of long-term finance, this continuing evolution has substantially reduced the strategic importance of access to informal sources which had played such an important part in the initial rise of a number of firms to positions of dominance.

Moreover, while many scholars now view the great merger wave as so transforming in its effects as to deserve the name of "Corporate Revolution," not all of them place equal emphasis upon the importance of the external changes in the structure of markets that the term implies. Alfred Chandler, for one, maintains that *internal* developments within firms were just as important as the external fact of merger, and indeed that administrative innovations after the 1890s were much more meaningful in the development of American business enterprise than legal ones. A legal consolidation became administratively consolidated only after its executive office began to do more than set price and production schedules. So long as decisions on how to produce and market, on how to allocate resources for the present and in the future, were left to the constituent enterprises the consolidation remained a mere federation of loosely allied units. It became administratively consolidated when the small executive office was transformed into a centralized headquarters that determined nearly all the activities of the firm's plants or marketing units and when the factories or sales offices, formerly managed by the heads of member firms, became operated by salaried plant managers or sales representatives.

Surely changes of these kinds improved the efficiency with which capital and labor were used. Surely they belong with economies of scale and other institutional changes among the prominent sources of productive efficiency in the modernized economy of the early twentieth century. In the next chapter we shall trace changes in business organization and techniques of managerial efficiency that took place in later years of the twentieth century, together with other main sources of productivity growth in the economy of today.

FOUR

The Technological Thrust
of the Twentieth Century

Before the early 1970s students of the American economy were deeply impressed by the growing efficiency with which resources were being used in the twentieth century. In contrast with land-and-resource-intensive techniques of production of earlier years, those of this century were clearly lessening the dependence of economic growth on the output of natural resources. Inputs of capital and labor were also being economized per unit of output. In a word, increases in output per capita were seen to be more and more responsive, *not* to increases in inputs of land, labor, and capital, but rather to the growing efficiency with which those inputs were being used.

This conclusion was firmly grounded on the rising significance of the role played by productivity gains in

115

increases in the Net National Product (NNP).* In the period 1840–90 productivity's contribution to NNP increases amounted to 17.3 percent. In the interval 1900–60 its contribution soared to 44.1 percent—well outdistancing the relative importance of contributions made by increases in supplies of land (2.5%), labor (34.8%), and capital stock (18.6%) to a rate of growth in NNP averaging 3.12 percent per year. According to Robert Gallman, in the nineteenth century about 50 percent of the rise in real per capita income was due to productivity gains. The corresponding figure thus far for the twentieth century is a whopping 80 percent!

The consequence has been an economic performance of unusual distinction. The measurements of Simon Kuznets show that NNP per capita in 1929–55 was about three times its level in the years 1869–88. This was indeed the "extraordinary achievement" that Kuznets called it. What made it even more so was the fact that the United States was practically unique in experiencing a rise of these proportions from levels that were already high in the initial period. To Gallman it was clear that "modern improvements in material well-being rest very prominently on gains in productivity." The "search for reasons for the success of the American economy," he added, "must be pursued with special vigor in this quarter." To be sure, it is no longer quite so clear that the successful achievements of even the recent past can be

---

*The Net National Product represents the value of goods and services produced during a given year, *minus* the value of the capital goods consumed in their production.

extended into the indefinite future. But before raising the question of the impact of recent and continuing shortages of raw materials and energy supplies on the future of economic growth, let us first examine changes in the sources of the gains that undeniably have been made.

It is technology, in the broadest sense of that word, that lies behind productivity gains. Technology consists in knowledge of ways to improve the relationship between inputs and outputs—that is, to "achieve more output with the same volume of resources, or the same output with a smaller volume of resources." These results can be achieved in numerous ways: for example, by the invention of new or improved machinery; advances in management and organizational technique; change in the design of factories to improve the flow of materials; improvements in work scheduling, personnel management, labor relations, methods of appraising and reaching potential markets, and many others.

Thus technological knowledge may take many forms. Knowledge, however, is not enough. If it is to affect productivity, it must issue in inventions or in improvements in organization and techniques that are adopted by numerous firms. The larger the number, the wider the diffusion of an innovation and the greater the impact on economic growth.

We have already seen how in the machine tool industry the phenomenon of "technological convergence" enabled innovations, skills, and techniques to spread from industry to industry between 1840 and 1910. Mechanization was probably the main source of new technology in the nineteenth century, and the widening of its range of application—the diffusion of a machine technology—was a principal vehicle for the technical progress of the century. That technology, however, owed relatively little to science. Rather, inventive activity was empirical and pragmatic, requiring little in the way of abstract thought or organized knowledge.

In the judgment of Nathan Rosenberg, the "shift in the composition of inventive activity away from the empirically-based and toward the newer science-based industries" is a distinctive feature of twentieth-century technology. This is not to suggest that the inventive process in the nineteenth century originated entirely in empiricism or that invention in the twentieth century is entirely scientific. Indeed, the trend toward reliance on science traces its roots to the second half of the nineteenth century. Yet it remains true that technological change has been increasingly dependent upon prior advances in systematized knowledge. Thus, while mechanization as a source of new technology continues with "great force" in the present century, according to Rosenberg, a succession of new sources has developed. And whether chemical, electrical, electronic, biological, or nuclear, the new sources have been "dependent upon the mastery of complex bodies of knowledge," none of which "could have been achieved by the crude empiricism and trial-and-error methods of earlier generations."

Rosenberg uses developments in metallurgy, especially those affecting the production of iron and steel, to illustrate the approach of the twentieth century to technological change. Prior to this century, technical progress in metallurgy, an activity fundamental to man's tool-making and tool-using abilities, had been based essentially on trial-and-error procedures. Nevertheless, it was still possible for important discoveries to be made so long as large numbers of individuals experimented with new techniques and materials. Metallurgical techniques could thus advance ahead of scientific understanding.

The discovery of the Bessemer process for converting iron into steel illustrates how this could occur. The success of Henry Bessemer's method depended on the use of ores free of phosphorus. However, he himself did not realize this. In his experiments he happened to use phosphorus-free Swedish charcoal iron. When the same technique was applied to British ores, which contained substantial amounts of phosphorus, it failed. The failure had a happy outcome, however. It led to prolonged, systematic study of the chemical processes involved in the making of iron and steel, and thus was a major event in the coming of the modern science of metallurgy.

Technological innovations in other spheres also made contributions of great importance to the conduct of metallurgical inquiry. The development of Henry Clifton Sorby's technique for examining metals under a microscope by the use of reflected light first made possible an understanding of the microstructure of steel, and later that of the nonferrous metals as well. The discovery and application of X-ray diffraction, and its use in the study of solids, revealed the structure of atomic particles and made its measurement possible. These improvements in experimental technique, originating in metallurgy, joined with and contributed to the emergence of a far broader and more fundamental understanding of the atomic and molecular structure of all matter.

The consequences of this "knowledge revolution" have been enormous. Once the general rules determining how atoms and molecules combine to form larger and more complex groups were mastered, it became possible, in Rosenberg's words, "to manipulate materials, to alter their characteristics, to maximize desirable properties, and even to create entirely new and synthetic materials with desired *combinations* of properties." In consequence, a number of new chemical-based industries have arisen which produce synthetic materials such as plastics, rubber and fibers, water-repellent coating, high-strength adhesives, and packaging materials out of combinations of properties which have no counterparts in the real world.

Rosenberg emphasizes that the basis for technical progress in these industries of the twentieth century is wholly different from the empirical foundations on which technological progress in the old metallurgical industries rested. The same may be said of the electronics industry, which, especially in the period after World War II, has made remarkable advances. Achievements such as the development of the transistor and the application of semiconductor devices to electronic data processing and to other military and commercial uses depended upon the development of quantum mechanics in the mid-1920s, as well as upon complex techniques for instrumentation.

Comparison between the nineteenth and twentieth centuries shows that agriculture as well as manufacturing has been transformed by the knowledge revolution. Because of the high land-labor ratio—the abundance of natural resources in relation to the population—a major problem confronting agriculture in the nineteenth century was to find ways of enabling a single farmer to cultivate larger acreages. Indeed, much of the innovation in the second half of the century had precisely that effect, with horse-drawn mechanical equipment replacing manpower in wide areas of farm work.

In agriculture as in manufacturing, mechanization played a key role in enabling large quantities of resources to be exploited with relatively little labor. In his study of the production of wheat, corn, and oats between 1840 and 1911, William N. Parker found that output per worker more than tripled, and he attributed to mechanization some 60 percent of the increase. Just two innovations, the reaper and thresher, were responsible for most (70%) of the contribution made by mechanization. In agriculture, as in early production of iron and steel, trial-and-error techniques prevailed, primarily taking the form of "a rather blind experimentation with seed varieties in new ecological environments, small variations in technique of planting and cultivation, and breeding methods that were haphazard or guided by mistaken principles." The basic biological processes involved were no more understood than were the chemical and physical properties underlying the science of metallurgy.

Whereas the main sources of increases in agricultural productivity in the nineteenth century were mechanization, transportation improvements, and regional crop specialization, the knowledge revolution of recent decades has placed particular emphasis upon genetics and biochemistry. So great have been resultant increases in output per worker that the proportion of the labor force in agriculture has fallen from 63 percent in 1840 to merely 8 percent in 1960. Other consequences are scarcely less revolutionary. Instead of adapting existing seed strains to the conditions of a given locality, it is now possible to create new strains possessing desired characteristics. Dependence upon specific natural resource inputs has been reduced; indeed, the productive contribution of land itself relative to purchased nonfarm inputs has been declining in recent decades.

Dependence on natural resources has been declining not only in agriculture but in industry as well. No clearer evidence of this decline can be presented than the following statistic on output of all resources—agricultural, timber products, and mineral—as a percentage of GNP. In 1870 that percentage was 36; in 1954 it was 12. Scarcities of particular resources during the major part of the twentieth century have been offset by growing skill in exploiting alternative resources in more abundant supply, by innovations that reduced resource requirements per unit of output, and by the development of synthetic materials. So successful were efforts of these kinds that as recently as 1972 Nathan Rosenberg could express the view that modern technology "may now be said to have displaced the primacy of natural resources in determining a country's growth prospects."

And since organized knowledge was, and remains, the crucial ingredient in modern technology, it is almost self-evident that education has played a vital role in the economic growth of the twentieth century. To be sure, there are difficulties in the way of measuring that role, and it must be acknowledged that careful study of the subject has only just begun. Counts of days and dollars spent on schooling are helpful but incomplete if we do not know what kind of schooling was given, and its quality. And even if we find answers to these kinds of questions it is by no means certain what kind of education has been most conducive to economic growth. Nor can we speak with certainty about the respective contributions to growth made by educated technological and managerial elites, on the one hand, and, on the other, by rising levels of educational achievement on the part of the population at large. Indeed, since educated persons are also usually people of native ability, we cannot be certain whether it is the education or the ability—nurture or nature, so to speak—that is responsible for the association observed nowadays between earned incomes and educational attainment.

These are questions of grave import and, having raised them, it is not our intent to set them aside in favor of statistics whose precise relevance is not yet determinable. Yet it is surely meaningful to record the fact that between the end of the nineteenth century and 1960 the average level of education rose from that of elementary school graduation to one where graduation from high school was typical. And it is surely meaningful to say that expenditures on education by federal, state, and local governments rose, in current dollars, from approximately $.25 billion in 1902 to nearly $23 billion in 1962, an increase well in excess both of changes in the level of prices and of the rate of population growth. Do rising levels of educational achievement and of per capita expenditures imply that in earlier years—say, those of the nineteenth century—education exercised a lesser influence on growth? That is almost certainly the case. As we have seen, technological change was largely empirical in its origins and, comparatively speaking, bodies of scientific knowledge on which invention might have drawn were too thin to require much sophistication in learning. In a word, earlier technological change required relatively little in the way of education beyond the ability to read and write.

In contrast, in the twentieth century, as Thomas C. Cochran has pointed out, "evolving technology in the plant and more complex business controls in the office" required care and guidance by "highly educated specialists." Particularly after World War II, he adds, big business came "to depend more and more on a supply of management personnel from graduating classes of the universities." In 1964, all but 24 percent of 1,000 executives in the largest 600 corporations had college or graduate degrees. Even in agriculture, Rosenberg suggests, "the sophisticated skills and decisions required of modern farmers make a university education highly desirable." It is scarcely surprising, then, that Edward F. Denison should have reached the suggestive if controversial conclusion that 23 percent of the growth of the national product between 1929 and 1957 is attributable to education. For investment in education creates the human capital—so-called because that investment, like other forms of capital, yields income payments—that is essential to the functioning of a technologically complex economy. Indeed, the more technologically progressive the economy, the greater the rate of return to education.

We conclude that the contribution of education to productivity change in this century is more important than in the last. For one thing, levels of expertise, both acquired and attained, have risen; for another, improvement in the average quality of the "human capital stock" has probably also occurred as a consequence of increased investment in education. But this is not to deny the importance of a high initial level of educational attainment on the adaptability and innovativeness of the population in the nineteenth century. It seems likely that this level was maintained by instruction in reading, writing, and mathematics, and that such instruction improved abilities to comprehend, follow directions, learn new techniques, and benefit by opportunities to better oneself. It is also likely, as Richard A. Easterlin has suggested, that education must have fostered "a view that problems may be solved by rational analyses and that it is possible to obtain control over one's environment." Impacts of these kinds are difficult to measure, but this is no reason for discounting them.

Because of the importance of technology to economic growth in the twentieth century one would expect to find a record of rising expenditures on research and development (R & D). The record does indeed show this, but given the purposes for which most such expenditures have been made, in general they have probably not yielded the impact on growth that a more ideal set of purposes would have allowed. Available estimates for selected years after 1920 indicate that R & D expenditures by government and private business have risen at a significantly higher rate than that of the Net National Product. The ratio more than doubled in the 1920s, doubled in the 1930s, and increased by one-half in the 1940s. In 1940, total outlays for R & D, financed in the main by private industry, amounted to about six-tenths of 1 percent of GNP. Expenditures by the federal government for R & D rose sharply during and after World War II, with the result that they amounted to fully 3 percent of GNP by the mid-1960s. In recent years almost two-thirds of all R & D expenditures have been financed by the federal government.

Most expenditures, however, have been devoted to development rather than basic research. Approximately two out of every three R & D dollars spent by the federal government have gone to development—with 90 percent of the outlays assigned to just three agencies: the Department of Defense, the National Aeronautic and Space Agency, and the Atomic Energy Commission. The record of private enterprise is even less impressive: in the second half of the 1960s less than 7 percent of its expenditures on R & D went to basic research. And if the purposes of the expenditures made by the federal government have been dominated by considerations of national security and prestige, those made by private business have been directed toward such modest objectives as annual changes in the design of consumer durables.

There are important exceptions to this generalization, however. Large firms in such science-based industries as chemicals and electronics are better able than small firms to afford funds for R & D. In addition, large firms are less wedded than firms in older industries to traditional products and markets, have less reason to seek to protect investments in existing technologies, and are hence more willing to take advantage of advances in scientific knowledge by manufacturing new products. Historically, manufacturing firms turned out a single product or at most a few closely related ones. Command over new technologies thus led to a diversification of product lines.

Internal R & D effort was not the only path to diversification. In numerous industries firms acquired new product lines by merging with the companies producing them. However achieved, diversification compelled changes in the organization and administration of business firms, and these changes made important, if immeasurable, contributions to productivity.

It was in the 1920s that leading companies in technologically advanced industries—electrical, automobile, chemical, and electronic—first adopted a strategy of growth via diversification into new lines of products. Following a route already charted by the Du Pont Company, they established large research departments and assigned them the task of bringing forth new goods as well as improving existing processes and products. United States Rubber, B. F. Goodrich, and other rubber companies began to exploit the potentials of rubber chemistry and to diversify their product lines. Electrical equipment manufacturers diversified into household appliances, and automobile manufacturers began to produce diesels and tractors. An important merger movement of the 1920s served as a vehicle for additional diversification, with the General Foods Company, for example, acquiring firms in practically every line of the food industry. Other mergers involved purchases of firms in distant and often completely unrelated lines. These so-called conglomerate mergers constituted approximately 20 percent of the total number effected in the years 1925–29.

The weak markets of the 1930s resulted in excess capacity, and this encouraged firms to continue their efforts to diversify their product lines. During World War II most firms were preoccupied by problems of conversion to military production and, later, with reconversion back to their old lines. Given the burgeoning markets and rapidly advancing technology of the postwar years, however, firms in metals, petroleum, and a number of other industries resumed the movement toward diversification. One result was a leap in the percentage of conglomerate mergers: from 21.0 percent in the years 1940–47, to 48.6 percent during 1951–55, and to 55.0 percent during 1956–60. By 1960, the vast majority of large manufacturers were producing goods in more than five separate industries, while over thirty giant companies manufactured in more than ten! Conglomerate mergers accounted for 60.0 percent of all mergers between 1961–65, then jumped to 81.6 percent for the years 1966–68.

Diversification created administrative problems that could not be handled by the highly centralized types of management structure that by the early 1900s had developed to supervise the production of single articles or product lines. It will be recalled that production, marketing, finance, and other functions were performed by specialized departments under the control of a central office. But, as the studies of Alfred D. Chandler, Jr., have shown: "the problems of obtaining materials and supplies, of manufacturing and of marketing a number of product lines for different parts of the world made the tasks of departmental headquarters exceedingly difficult to administer systematically and rationally."

Coordination by the central office of product flow through the several departments proved even more formidable. Essentially, the problem was to analyze intelligently a host of economic functions—including engineering and research as well as production, distribution, transportation, procurement of supplies, and finance—when the appraisals had to be made in several very different industries or lines of business. Furthermore, the making of long-term strategic plans not only required decisions bearing on the future use of existing facilities, personnel, and funds, and the development of new resources in the company's current lines, but also required decisions having to do with new lines of products and with the dropping or curtailing of old ones.

The answer was to decentralize, to set up a division for each product or product line and make that division responsible for all activities. These autonomous operating divisions, in turn, were placed under the administrative control of a general office. In the 1920s, Du Pont, General Motors, Sears, and Jersey Standard pioneered in the development of the decentralized, multidivision, general office type of structure. By 1960 the structure had become the accepted form of management for the most complex and diverse of American industrial enterprises.

These organizational and administrative changes

have enabled resources to be economized per unit of output and thus have contributed to the growth of productivity. Freed from all but the most essential entrepreneurial duties, the executives in the general office are far better able to concentrate on long-term strategies for growth and expansion, better able to determine whether a new product created by the research department uses enough of the firm's present resources, or will help sufficiently in the development of new ones to warrant its production and sale. Similarly, they can better decide whether or not to go into new product lines, to set up new divisions for their production and sale, or to incorporate these activities into an already extant division that is closely related to the new lines. In sum, their essential functions are to coordinate, appraise, and determine general policy.

In addition, procedures for improving internal controls have been developed. These include an increase in middle-management personnel and greater use of specialized staff consultants; interdivisional billing at the going market price (which sharpens competition between divisions); improved accounting and cost-control procedures; and devices to speed the flow of information essential to decision making. By these and other means modern corporate administrations seek to rationalize operations, reduce unit costs, expand output and sales, and grow at the expense of rivals. It cannot be too much emphasized, however, that carefully designed systems of organization and administration, maximum use of numerical data and computers, and employment of highly educated specialists as staff consultants to study and improve operations, provide no automatic guarantees that wise decisions will be made. The most important business problems and opportunities continue to require the exercise of human judgment—and always will.

Nevertheless, the productivity-enhancing effects of modern technology—which, once again, include the organizational and administrative advances we have just discussed—have been truly impressive, and there is scarcely a nation in the world that would turn its back on the betterment of living standards that it has made possible. This does not mean that great business empires promote efficiency and growth more decisively than smaller specialized firms. While it is difficult to be certain, they well may not. Nor does this mean that poverty has been erased from the American scene. Of course it has not. What is more, that it ever will be is unlikely. Perhaps no truer words were ever written than those of the Bible: "The poor ye have always with you."

The reason for this is that poverty, whether defined in *The Other America* by Michael Harrington or by a presidential Income Maintenance Commission, is measured by Americans not in absolute but relative terms. As Stanley Lebergott has pointed out, "Poverty is what afflicts Americans who fall behind today's here-and-now standard of living." In the words of Harrington: "The American poor are not poor . . . in the sixteenth century; they are poor here and now in the United States. They are dispossessed in terms of what the rest of the nation enjoys. . . . They watch the movies and read the magazines of affluent Americans, and these tell them that they are internal exiles."

In *absolute* terms, the percentage of American families below the official poverty line, as defined by the Office of Economic Opportunity, has fallen since 1936 from 56 percent to less than 10 percent. Even allowing for inflation, the "average" income of the bottom tenth of the population has gone up about 55 percent since 1950. The typical "poor" family of today can buy as much food as the average American worker could buy in his grandparents' time, and, in addition, better housing, more clothing, furniture, heat, and medical care. Forty-one percent of our officially poor families own automobiles. Half a million own more than one car. In any absolute sense, then, America's economic growth has increased the level of material well-being of the "average" family. Yet because increasing affluence has led society to elevate its notions of what constitutes poverty, the relative position of the poor has changed hardly at all.

Needless to say, however, some families are more "average" than others. Even among the bottom tenth, not all ethnic and racial groups have fared equally well in the distribution of the absolute benefits of economic growth. Blacks make up a large proportion of those considerable numbers of poor people who are employed as domestics or in jobs of low productivity and pay. This is a legacy of slavery and of inadequate postwar investment in education. Thus, although slavery was profitable in the short run, it generated long-run costs. The history of the nation must record not only the profits of antebellum planters but also the tragic wastage of human capital. The Great Keeper of long-term profit and loss accounts sometimes makes surprising deductions from the short-run gains men reckon. Discrimination grievously continues to block equal access to qualitatively superior education and then fastens on resultant educational deficiencies to justify the tendering of jobs that are inconsonant with human dignity. The vicious circle must be broken again and again. Economic growth has helped, but not enough.

While economic growth has reduced poverty in the absolute sense, it has come under increasing attack as an objective worthy of pursuit. Some critics argue that the limits of growth are set by finite global supplies of natural resources and sources of energy, and recently revealed worldwide shortages of raw materials and energy underline the point. The scenario of these critics is grim: if world consumption of oil continues to increase at current rates of use (about 10 percent of existing reserves per annum), these reserves—including projected future discoveries—figure to be exhausted in about twenty years. The same timetable applies to such vital elements as silver, gold, copper, lead, platinum, tin, and zinc. Other critics include population growth and food shortages in their calculations, and while differing on the date of Armageddon, agree on the inevitability of its coming. Thus, rising demand for resources will outrun supply, and growth will peter out in widespread depletion of its sinews.

Perhaps it will. But then again perhaps it will not. Depletionist critics of growth assume that the world economy is incapable of adjusting to shortages in materials and resources. As Peter Passell and Leonard Ross point out in a recent effort to countermand the *Retreat from Riches*, the assumption largely reflects the omission of the variable of prices in projections of how resources will be used. When resources are scarce in relation to the demand for them, their price rises, and this induces users to substitute cheaper materials. Higher prices both stimulate efforts to conserve resource inputs and increase their supply through exploration.

The fact of the matter is that while there are exceptions in the case of some materials, the relative prices of natural resources as a class have not risen historically. Hence, the record of the past gives little evidence that the growth of the industrialized world is pressing against rigid raw material supply constraints. Mineral prices have roughly kept pace with industrial prices for the last one hundred years. The reasons for this are clear. In spite of the scarcity of high-grade ores, technical change has dramatically reduced costs of exploration and extraction. And technology has widened the opportunities to substitute plentiful materials for scarce ones.

The price rises of the recent past may well provide the needed incentive for efforts to speed the pace of substitution and, in addition, to discover and develop new sources of energy. Petroleum and natural gas will surely have to be supplemented by other energy sources in the near future. In a recent study on "The Allocation of Energy Resources" (February 1974) William D. Nordhaus predicts that domestic petroleum resources will be virtually exhausted by 1980, and that imported petroleum and natural gas will put a heavy drain on the United States balance of payments—besides being liable to interruption from political causes. After the year 2000, Nordhaus believes, the importance of imported energy sources will diminish, and that of liquefied coal and shale oil, augmented by light-water nuclear reactors, will grow. As the twenty-first century wears on, the breeder reactor will gradually take over; and solar, geothermal, gravitational, and perhaps other, as yet unforeseeable, new energy technologies may emerge to supplement it. After the exhaustion of the fossil fuels, perhaps in the twenty-second century, the economy will have to run on an electric hydrogen technology or some other exotic technology with a resource base that is virtually infinite, if high industrial civilizations are to survive. Nordhaus is optimistic. In his opinion, "we should not be haunted by the specter of the affluent society grinding to a halt for a lack of energy resources."

Nevertheless, there are some who believe that technical progress will not keep pace with the pressures exerted by economic growth on agricultural and mineral resources and on the environment. These stresses, they argue, tend to multiply geometrically (or, in the language of mathematics, exponentially) while the capability of technical progress of accommodating to these rising demands is far more narrowly limited. The argument is basically similar to ideas expressed two centuries ago by the Reverend Thomas Malthus. Malthus's point was that since people tend to multiply exponentially, while, at best, the food supply increases at a constant rate, only continence, war, and starvation can redress the balance. Admittedly, the quality of life in the future will probably depend on willingness to slow rates of population growth. Yet one cannot avoid the conclusion that since the days of Malthus technological advance has, at the very least, helped postpone the confrontation between humanity and the resources of the world. And while, as Passell and Ross acknowledge, no one can be certain about it, technical progress does not seem to be slowing down; indeed, the "best econometric estimates" indicate that it is growing exponentially.

Those critics of economic growth who deplore the effects of technological progress on the environment are on firmer ground. Among the "external diseconomies" of growth, particularly since the end of World War II, are air pollution, water pollution, solid waste pollution, congestion, noise, decline in security of persons and property, and general uglification of town and country. Highly productive factories use river water as a coolant, then dump it back "warmed and reeking with chemicals." Synthetic insecticides increase crop yields but are washed off millions of farms into the national water supply—threatening to make fish toxic to man. Electric power plants generate energy cheaply and efficiently, yet join with garbage incinerators and automobiles to foul the air of the nation's cities. Since the end of World War II the production of deadly mercury waste has increased dramatically, mainly because of the demand for chlorine. Tough plastic packaging, unlike frail cardboard, is impervious to chemical breakdown, so that litter remains intact until somebody picks it up. Phosphorus and nitrogen compounds from laundry detergents, processed sewage, and fertilizers are pumped into lakes and rivers, where they disrupt the balance of animal and vegetable life in large lakes. In consequence, some kinds of fish have disappeared altogether from Lake Erie, for example, and all catches are down sharply. The indictment, carefully drawn by Passell and Ross, could be expanded.

But is economic growth at fault? Or deficiencies in public policy? Economists answer that pollution comes not from growth but from "our perverse system of incentives to industry." And that is our answer too. Firms have been encouraged to poison the air and foul the water because society has regarded the environment as a free good. Now that pure air and water are becoming scarcer goods, society must insist that firms pay for their use. Taxation can compel firms to "internalize" social costs of production that were previously hidden or obscured. But since these costs will then be included among other costs of production, prices of goods and services must rise in consequence. Passell and Ross suggest that "halting growth would do far less to scrub the environment than a simple policy of making business put its money where its exhaust is." We should add to this that consumers must also be willing to pay the higher prices that must result. If they truly value environmental quality they will be willing to do so.

Meanwhile it may be we will be best advised to adopt an attitude of watchful optimism with respect to the promise of economic growth. We know that it has reduced absolute poverty, that its historically growing need for improvement in the quality of human capital has been among the vital influences making for a truer social democracy. All benefits have their costs, and American society must be vigilant in its efforts to balance the one against the other. Like Cassandra, one may foresee a sputtering of light and an enfeeblement of effort in consequence of some future running down of the sources of energy. Or, like Prometheus unbound, look to the possibility of controlled nuclear fusion for all the energy the planet will need for several billion years. The future, perhaps the near future, will sift degrees of right and wrong in expectations regarding these problems that may reflect differences in temperament more than those of knowledge.

SELECTED BIBLIOGRAPHY

BOOKS

Andreano, Ralph, ed. *The Economic Impact of the American Civil War*. 2nd ed. Cambridge, Mass.: Schenkman Publishing Company, 1967.

Atherton, Lewis E. *The Southern Country Store, 1800–1860*. Baton Rouge, La.: Louisiana State University Press, 1949.

Barger, Harold. *The Transportation Industries, 1889–1946: A Study of Output, Employment and Productivity*. New York: National Bureau of Economic Research, 1951.

———, and H. H. Landsberg. *American Agriculture, 1899–1939: A Study in Output, Employment and Productivity*. New York: National Bureau of Economic Research, 1942.

Berg, Ivar, ed. *Human Resources and Economic Welfare: Essays in Honor of Eli Ginzberg*. New York: Columbia University Press, 1972.

Bidwell, Percy W., and John I. Falconer. *History of Agriculture in the Northern United States, 1620–1860*. Originally published 1925; reprinted New York: Peter Smith, 1941.

Blair, John M. *Economic Concentration: Structure, Behavior, and Public Policy*. New York: Harcourt, Brace, Jovanovich, 1972.

Bogue, Allan G. *From Prairie to Corn Belt: Farming on the Illinois and Iowa Prairies in the Nineteenth Century*. Chicago: University of Chicago Press, 1963.

139

Brady, Dorothy, ed. *Output, Employment, and Productivity in the United States After 1800.* Conference on Research in Income and Wealth, National Bureau of Economic Research. Vol. 30, *Studies in Income and Wealth.* New York: Columbia University Press, 1966.

Brownlee, W. Elliot. *Dynamics of Ascent: A History of the American Economy.* New York: Alfred A. Knopf, 1974.

Bruchey, Stuart. *The Roots of American Economic Growth, 1607–1860: An Essay in Social Causation.* New York: Harper and Row, 1965.

———, ed. *Cotton and the Growth of the American Economy.* New York: Harcourt, Brace and World, 1967.

Buck, Norman S. *The Development of the Organization of Anglo-American Trade, 1800–1859.* New Haven: Yale University Press, 1925.

Chandler, Alfred D., Jr. *Strategy and Structure: Chapters in the History of American Industrial Enterprise.* Cambridge, Mass.: M.I.T. Press, 1962.

———, ed. *Giant Enterprise: Ford, General Motors, and the Automobile Industry.* New York: Harcourt, Brace and World, 1964.

———, ed. *The Railroads: The Nation's First Big Business.* New York: Harcourt, Brace and World, 1965.

———, and Stephen Salsbury. *Pierre S. DuPont and the Making of the Modern Corporation.* New York: Harper and Row, 1971.

Clark, John G. *The Grain Trade in the Old Northwest.* Urbana, Ill.: University of Illinois Press, 1966.

Clark, Victor S. *History of American Manufactures.* 3 vols. Originally published 1929; reprinted New York: Peter Smith, 1949.

Coale, Ansley J., and Melvin Zelnik. *New Estimates of Fertility and Population in the United States.* Princeton: Princeton University Press, 1963.

Cochran, Thomas C. *American Business in the Twentieth Century.* Cambridge, Mass.: Harvard University Press, 1972.

———. *The American Business System: An Historical Perspective, 1900–1955.* Cambridge, Mass.: Harvard University Press, 1955.

———. *Business and American Life: A History.* New York: Mc Graw-Hill, 1972.

———, and William Miller. *The Age of Enterprise: A Social History of Industrial America.* Originally published 1942; reprinted New York: Harper and Brothers, 1961.

Conference on Economic Progress. *Poverty and Deprivation in the United States.* Washington, D.C.: The Conference, 1962.

Conrad, Alfred H., and John R. Meyer. *The Economics of Slavery.* Chicago: Aldine, 1964.

Danhof, Clarence H. *Change in Agriculture: The Northern United States, 1820–1870.* Cambridge, Mass.: Harvard University Press, 1969.

Davis, Lance E., and Douglass C. North. *Institutional Change and American Economic Growth.* Cambridge, Eng.: Cambridge University Press, 1971.

Denison, Edward F. *The Sources of Economic Growth in the United States and the Alternatives Before Us.* New York: Committee for Economic Development, 1962.

Dewey, Donald. *Monopoly in Economics and Law.* Chicago: Rand, McNally, 1959.

Evans, G. Heberton, Jr. *Business Incorporations in the United States, 1800–1943.* New York: National Bureau of Economic Research, 1948.

Fishlow, Albert. *American Railroads and the Transformation of the Antebellum Economy.* Cambridge, Mass.: Harvard University Press, 1965.

Fogel, Robert William. *Railroads and American Economic Growth: Essays in Econometric History.* Baltimore: Johns Hopkins Press, 1964.

———, and Stanley L. Engerman. *Time on the Cross.* 2 vols. I: *The Economics of American Negro Slavery.* New York: Little, Brown, 1974.

———, eds. *The Reinterpretation of American Economic History.* New York: Harper and Row, 1971.

Frickey, Edwin. *Production in the United States, 1860–1914.* Cambridge, Mass.: Harvard University Press, 1947.

Friedman, Milton, and Anna J. Swartz. *A Monetary History of the United States, 1867–1960.* Princeton: Princeton University Press, 1963.

Galambos, Louis. *Competition and Cooperation: The Emergence of a National Trade Association.* Baltimore: Johns Hopkins Press, 1966.

Garraty, John A. *The New Commonwealth, 1877–1890.* New York: Harper and Row, 1968.

Gates, Paul W. *The Farmer's Age: Agriculture, 1815–1860.* New York: Holt, Rinehart and Winston, 1951.

———. *History of Public Land Law Development.* Written for the Public Land Law Review Commission. Washington, D. C.: Government Printing Office, November, 1968.

Gibb, George S. *The Saco-Lowell Shops: Textile Machinery Building in New England, 1813–1949.* Cambridge, Mass.: Harvard University Press, 1950.

Gilchrist, David T., and W. David Lewis, eds. *Economic Change in the Civil War Era.* Greenville, Del.: Eleutherian Mills-Hagley Foundation, 1965.

Glaab, Charles N., and T. Brown. *A History of Urban America.* New York: Macmillan and Company, 1967.

Gray, Lewis C. *History of Agriculture in the Southern United States to 1860.* 2 vols. Originally published in 1933; reprinted Gloucester, Mass.: Peter Smith, 1958.

Goldsmith, Raymond W. *Financial Intermediaries in the American Economy Since 1900.* Princeton: Princeton University Press, 1958.

———. *A Study of Savings in the United States.* Princeton: Princeton University Press, 1955.

Habbakkuk, H. J. *American and British Technology in the Nineteenth Century.*

Cambridge, Eng.: Cambridge University Press, 1962.

Hammond, Bray. *Banks and Politics in America from the Revolution to the Civil War.* Princeton: Princeton University Press, 1957.

Harrington, Michael. *The Other America.* New York: Macmillan and Company, 1962.

Hays, Samuel P. *Conservation and the Gospel of Efficiency: The Progressive Conservation Movement, 1890–1920.* Cambridge, Mass.: Harvard University Press, 1959.

Helfrich, H. W., ed. *The Environmental Crisis.* New Haven: Yale University Press, 1970.

Hidy, Ralph W., and Muriel E. Hidy. *Pioneering in Big Business, 1882–1911.* New York: Harper and Brothers, 1955.

Hunter, Louis C. *Steamboats on the Western Rivers.* Cambridge, Mass.: Harvard University Press, 1949.

Hurst, James Willard. *Law and the Conditions of Freedom in the Nineteenth Century United States.* Madison: University of Wisconsin Press, 1964.

Johnson, Arthur M. *The Development of American Petroleum Pipelines: A Study in Private Enterprise and Public Policy, 1862–1906.* Ithaca, N.Y.: Cornell University Press, 1956.

———, and Barry E. Supple. *Boston Capitalists and Western Railroads: A Study in the Nineteenth Century Investment Process.* Cambridge, Mass.: Harvard University Press, 1967.

Jones, Fred M. *Middlemen in the Domestic Trade of the United States, 1800–1860.* Illinois Studies in the Social Sciences. Vol. 21, no. 3. Urbana: University of Illinois Press, 1937.

Kaysen, Carl, and Donald F. Turner. *Antitrust Policy: An Economic and Legal Analysis.* Cambridge, Mass.: Harvard University Press, 1959.

Kelsey, Darwin P., ed. *Farming in the New Nation: Interpreting American Agriculture, 1790–1840.* Washington, D.C.: The Agricultural History Society, 1972.

Kendrick, John W. *Postwar Productivity Trends in the United States, 1948–1969.* National Bureau of Economic Research. New York: Columbia University Press, 1973.

———. *Productivity Trends in the United States.* Princeton: Princeton University Press, 1961.

Kirkland, Edward C. *Industry Comes of Age: Business, Labor and Public Policy, 1860–1897.* New York: Holt, Rinehart and Winston, 1961.

———. *Men, Cities, and Transportation: A Study in New England History, 1800–1920.* Cambridge, Mass.: Harvard University Press, 1948.

Kuznets, Simon. *Capital in the American Economy: Its Formation and Financing.* Princeton: Princeton University Press, 1961.

———. *Modern Economic Growth: Rate, Structure and Spread.* New Haven: Yale University Press, 1966.

———. *National Income: A Summary of Findings.* New York: National Bureau of Economic Research, 1946.

——. *National Income and Its Composition, 1919–1938.* New York: National Bureau of Economic Research, 1954.

——. *Postwar Economic Growth: Four Lectures.* Cambridge, Mass.: Belknap Press of Harvard University Press, 1964.

Lampman, Robert J. *Changes in the Share of Wealth by Top Wealth-Holders, 1922–1956.* New York: National Bureau of Economic Research, 1960.

Lebergott, Stanley. *Manpower in Economic Growth: The United States Record Since 1800.* New York: McGraw-Hill and Company, 1964.

Mason, Edward S., ed. *The Corporation in Modern Society.* Cambridge, Mass.: Harvard University Press, 1959.

Miller, Herman P. *Poverty, American Style.* Belmont, Calif.: Wadsworth, 1966.

Misham, E. J. *The Costs of Economic Growth.* Harmondsworth, Eng.: Penguin, 1969.

Nash, Roderick, ed. *The American Environment: Readings in the History of Conservation.* Reading, Mass.: Addison-Wesley, 1968.

Nelson, Ralph L. *Merger Movements in American Industry.* Princeton: Princeton University Press, 1959.

Nevins, Allan. *Study in Power: John D. Rockefeller, Industrialist and Philanthropist.* New York: Charles Scribner's Sons, 1953.

Nordhaus, William, and James Tobin. *Economic Growth.* National Bureau of Economic Research: *Fifteenth Anniversary Colloquium V.* New York: Columbia University Press, 1972.

North, Douglass C. *The Economic Growth of the United States, 1790–1860.* Englewood Cliffs, N.J.: Prentice-Hall, 1961.

——. *Growth and Welfare in the American Past.* Englewood Cliffs, N.J.: Prentice-Hall, 1966.

Parker, William N., ed. *Trends in the American Economy in the Nineteenth Century.* Conference on Research in Income and Wealth. National Bureau of Economic Research Vol. 24, *Studies in Income and Wealth.* Princeton: Princeton University Press, 1960.

Passell, Peter, and Leonard Ross. *The Retreat from Riches: Affluence and Its Enemies.* New York: Viking Press, 1973.

Passer, Harold C. *The Electrical Manufacturers, 1875–1900: A Study in Competition, Entrepreneurship, Technical Change, and Economic Growth.* Cambridge, Mass.: Harvard University Press, 1953.

Perloff, Harvey S., et al. *Regions, Resources and Economic Growth.* Baltimore: Johns Hopkins Press, 1960.

Redlich, Fritz. *The Molding of American Banking: Men and Ideas.* Part II, *1840–1910.* New York: Hafner Publishing Company, 1951.

Rogin, Leo. *The Introduction of Farm Machinery in Its Relation to the Productivity of Labor in the Agriculture of the United States during the Nineteenth Century.* Berkeley: University of California Press, 1931.

Rosenberg, Nathan. *Technology and American Economic Growth.* New York: Harper and Row, 1973.

———, ed. *The American System of Manufactures.* Edinburgh: Edinburgh University Press, 1969.

Schmookler, Jacob. *Invention and Economic Growth.* Cambridge, Mass.: Harvard University Press, 1966.

Scoville, James G., ed. *Perspectives on Poverty and Income Distribution.* Lexington, Mass.: D. C. Heath, 1971.

Shannon, Fred A. *The Farmer's Last Frontier: Agriculture, 1860–1897.* New York: Holt, Rinehart and Winston, 1945.

Stampp, Kenneth M. *The Peculiar Institution: Slavery in the Antebellum South.* New York: Alfred A. Knopf, 1956.

Stover, John F. *American Railroads.* Chicago: University of Chicago Press, 1961.

———. *Railroads of the South, 1865–1900: A Study in Finance and Control.* Chapel Hill: University of North Carolina Press, 1955.

Strassmann, W. Paul. *Risk and Technological Innovation: American Manufacturing Methods during the Nineteenth Century.* Ithaca, N.Y.: Cornell University Press, 1959.

Taeuber, Conrad, and Irene B. Taeuber. *The Changing Population of the United States.* New York: John Wiley, 1958.

Taeuber, K. E., and A. F. Taeuber. *Negroes in Cities.* Chicago: Aldine, 1965.

Taylor, George Rogers. *The Transportation Revolution, 1815–1860.* New York: Holt, Rinehart and Winston, 1951.

Temin, Peter. *Iron and Steel in Nineteenth Century America: An Economic Inquiry.* Cambridge, Mass.: M.I.T. Press, 1964.

———. *The Jacksonian Economy.* New York: W. W. Norton, 1969.

Thernstrom, Stephan, and Richard Sennett. *Nineteenth Century Cities: Essays in the New Urban History.* New Haven: Yale University Press, 1969.

Thorelli, Hans B. *Federal Antitrust Policy: The Origination of an American Tradition.* Baltimore: Johns Hopkins Press, 1955.

United States Department of Labor and United States Department of Commerce. *Social and Economic Condition of Negroes in the United States.* Washington, D. C.: Govenment Printing Office, 1967.

Usher, Abbott P. *A History of Mechanical Invention.* Cambridge, Mass.: Harvard University Press, 1954.

Van Fenstermaker, J. *The Development of American Commercial Banking, 1782–1837.* Kent, Ohio: Kent State University Press, 1965.

Vatter, Harold G. *The United States Economy in the 1950's.* New York: W. W. Norton Company, 1963.

Ward, Barbara, et al., eds. *The Widening Gap: Development in the 1970's.* New York: Columbia University Press, 1971.

Ware, Caroline F. *The Early New England Cotton Manufacture.* Boston: Houghton Mifflin Company, 1931.

Wilkins, Mira. *The Emergence of Multinational Enterprise: American Business Abroad from the Colonial Era to 1914.* Cambridge, Mass.: Harvard University Press, 1970.

Williamson, Harold F., and Arnold R. Daum. *The American Petroleum Industry: The Age of Illumination, 1859–1899.* Evanston, Ill.: Northwestern University Press, 1959.

Williamson, Jeffrey G. *American Growth and the Balance of Payments, 1820–1913.* Chapel Hill: University of North Carolina Press, 1964.

Woodman, Harold D. *King Cotton and His Retainers: Financing and Marketing the Cotton Crop of the South, 1800–1925.* Lexington, Ky.: University of Kentucky Press, 1968.

Yasuba, Yasukichi. *Birth Rates of the White Population of the United States, 1800–1860.* Baltimore: Johns Hopkins Press, 1961.

ARTICLES AND BOOK CHAPTERS

Abramovitz, Moses. "Manpower, Capital, and Technology." In *Human Resources and Economic Welfare: Essays in Honor of Eli Ginzberg.* Ed. Ivar Berg. New York: Columbia University Press, 1972.

——. "Resource and Output Trends in the United States Since 1870." American Economic Review, *Papers and Proceedings,* 46 (May 1956), 5–23.

——, and Paul A. David. "Reinterpreting Economic Growth: Parables and Realities." *American Economic Review,* 63, no. 2 (May 1973), 428–439.

Adelman, Morris A. "The Measurement of Industrial Concentration." *Review of Economics and Statistics,* 33 (November 1951), 269–296.

Ames, Edward, and Nathan Rosenberg. "The Enfield Arsenal in Theory and History." *The Economic Journal,* 78, no. 312 (December 1968), 827–842.

Bruchey, Stuart. "The Business Economy of Marketing Change." In *Farming in the New Nation: Interpreting American Agriculture, 1790–1840.* Ed. Darwin P. Kelsey. Washington, D.C.: The Agricultural History Society, 1972.

——. "Corporation—Historical Development." In *Encyclopaedia Britannica* (1963 edition).

Chandler, Alfred D., Jr. "Anthracite Coal and the Beginnings of the Industrial Revolution in the United States." *Business History Review,* 46 (Summer 1972), 141–181.

——. "The Structure of American Industry in the Twentieth Century: An Historical Overview." *Business History Review,* 43, (Autumn 1969), 255–298.

Cochran, Thomas C. "Did the Civil War Retard Industrialization?" In *The Economic Impact of the American Civil War.* Ed. Ralph Andreano.

2nd ed. Cambridge, Mass: Schenkman Publishing Company, 1967.

Conrad, Alfred H., et al. "Slavery as an Obstacle to Economic Growth in the United States: A Panel Discussion." *Journal of Economic History,* 27 (December 1967), 518–560.

David, Paul A. "The Growth of Real Product in the United States before 1840: New Evidence and Controlled Conjecture." *Journal of Economic History,* 27 (June 1967), 151–197.

———. "The Landscape and the Machine." In *Essays on a Mature Economy: Britain After 1840.* Ed. D. M. McCloskey. London: Methuen, 1971.

———. "Learning by Doing and Tariff Protection: A Reconsideration of the Case of the Ante-Bellum United States Cotton Textile Industry." *Journal of Economic History,* 30 (September 1970), 521–601.

———. "The Mechanization of Reaping in the Ante-Bellum Midwest." In *The Reinterpretation of American Economic History.* Ed. Robert W. Fogel and Stanley L. Engerman. New York: Harper and Row, 1971. Pp. 214–227.

———. "Towards Historically Relevant Parables of Growth." Stanford Research Center in Economic Growth, Memo. 122, November 1971.

———, and Peter Temin. "Capitalist Masters, Bourgeois Slaves." In M.I.T. Department of Economics Working Paper No. 134, July 1974.

———, and Peter Temin. "Slavery: The Progressive Institution?" Stanford Research Center in Economic Growth, Memo. 171, June 1974.

Davis, Lance E. "Banks and Their Economic Effects." In *American Economic Growth.* Ed. Lance E. Davis et al. New York: Harper and Row, 1972. Pp. 340–368.

———. "Capital and Growth." In ibid. Pp. 280–310.

———. "Capital Immobilities and Finance Capitalism: A Study of Economic Evolution inthe United States, 1820–1920." In *Purdue Faculty Papers in Economic History, 1956–1966.* Homewood, Ill.: Irwin, 1967.

———. "Savings Sources and Utilization." In *American Economic Growth.* Ed. Lance E. Davis et al. New York: Harper and Row, 1972. Pp. 311–339.

———, and H. Louis Stettler III. "The New England Textile Industy, 1825–60; Trends and Fluctuations." In *Output, Employment, and Productivity in the United States After 1800.* Ed. Dorothy Brady. Conference on Research in Income and Wealth, National Bureau of Economic Research. Vol. 30, *Studies in Income and Wealth.* New York: Columbia University Press, 1966. Pp. 213–242.

Domar, Evsey D. "On the Measurement of Comparative Efficiency." In *Comparison of Economic Systems: Theoretical and Methodological Approaches.* Ed. A. Eckstein. Berkeley: University of California Press, 1971.

———. "On the Measurement of Technological Change." *The Economic Journal,* 71 (December 1961), 709–729.

Easterlin, R. A. "The American Population." In *American Economic Growth.* Ed. Lance E. Davis et al. New York: Harper and Row, 1972. Pp. 121–183.

———. "Interregional Differences in Per Capita Income, Population, and Total Income, 1840–1950." In *Trends in the American Economy in the Nineteenth Century.* Ed. William N. Parker. Conference on Research in Income and Wealth, National Bureau of Economic Research. Vol. 24, *Studies in Income and Wealth.* Princeton: Princeton University Press, 1960, Pp. 73–140.

Eichner, Alfred S. "Business Concentration and Its Significance." In *The Business of America.* Ed. Ivar Berg. New York: Harcourt, Brace and World, 1968. Pp. 169–200.

Engerman, Stanley L. "The Effects of Slavery upon the Southern Economy." *Explorations in Entrepreneurial History,* 4 (Winter 1967), 71–97.

Fishlow, Albert. "The Common School Revival: Fact or Fancy?" In *Industrialization in Two Systems.* Ed. Henry Rosovsky. New York: John Wiley, 1966. Pp. 40–67.

———. "Internal Transportation." In *American Economic Growth.* Ed. Lance E. Davis et al. New York: Harper and Row, 1972. Pp. 486–547.

———. "Levels of Nineteenth-Century American Investment in Education." *Journal of Economic History,* 26 (December 1966), 418–436.

———. "Productivity and Technological Change in the Railroad Sector." In *Output, Employment, and Productivity in the United States after 1800.* Ed. Dorothy Brady. Conference on Research in Income and Wealth, National Bureau of Economic Research. Vol. 30, *Studies in Income and Wealth.* New York: Columbia University Press, 1966. Pp. 583–646.

Foust, James D., and Dale E. Swan. "Productivity and Profitability of Antebellum Slave Labor: A Micro Approach." In *The Structure of the Cotton Economy of the Antebellum South.* Ed. William N. Parker. Washington, D.C.: Agricultural History Society, 1970. Pp. 39–62.

Gallman, Robert E. "Commodity Output, 1839–1899." In *Trends in the American Economy in the Nineteenth Century.* Conference on Research in Income and Wealth, National Bureau of Economic Research. Vol. 24, *Studies in Income and Wealth.* Princeton: Princeton University Press, 1960. Pp. 13–72.

———. "Fundamental Concepts of Statistical Studies as Applied to Economic History." In *Approaches to Economic History.* Eds. George Rogers Taylor and Lucius F. Ellsworth. Charlottesville: University of Virginia Press, 1971.

———. "Gross National Product in the United States, 1834–1909." In *Output, Employment, and Productivity in the United States after 1800.* Ed. Dorothy Brady. Conference on Research in Income and Wealth, National Bureau of Economic Research. Vol. 30, *Studies in Income and Wealth.* New York: Columbia University Press, 1966. Pp. 3–76.

———. "The Pace and Pattern of American Economic Growth." In *American Economic Growth.* Ed. Lance E. Davis et al. New York: Harper and Row, 1972. Pp. 15–60.

———. "Trends in the Size Distribution of Wealth in the Nineteenth Century: Some Speculations." In *Six Papers on the Size Distribution of Wealth and Income.* Ed. Lee Soltow. New York: National Bureau of Economic Research, 1969.

———, and Lance E. Davis. "The Share of Savings and Investment in Gross National Product During the Nineteenth Century, United States of America." Stanford Research Center in Economic Growth, Memo. 63, July 1968.

Lampard, Eric E. "The Evolving System of Cities in the United States: Urbanization and Economic Development." In *Issues in Urban Economics.* Eds. Harvey S. Perloff and Lowdon Wingo, Jr. Baltimore: Johns Hopkins Press, 1968.

Lebergott, Stanley. "The American Labor Force." In *American Economic Growth.* Ed. Lance E. Davis. New York: Harper and Row, 1972. Pp. 184–232.

———. "Can American Capitalism End Poverty?" Unpublished manuscript.

———. "Labor Force and Employment, 1800–1960." In *Output, Employment, and Productivity in the United States After 1800.* Ed. Dorothy Brady. Conference on Research in Income and Wealth, National Bureau of Economic Research. Vol. 30, *Studies in Income and Wealth.* New York: Columbia University Press, 1966. Pp. 117–204.

———. "United States Transport Advance and Externalities." *Journal of Economic History.* 26 (December 1966), 437–461.

Lorant, John H. "Technological Change in American Manufacturing During the 1920's." *Journal of Economic History,* 27 (June 1967), 243–246.

Main, Jackson T. "Trends in Wealth Concentration Before 1860." *Journal of Economic History,* 31 (June 1971), 445–447.

McClelland, Peter D. "Railroads, American Growth, and the New Economic History: A Critique." *Journal of Economic History,* 28 (March 1968), 102–123.

Meeker, Edward. "The Improving Health of the United States, 1850–1915." *Explorations in Economic History,* 9 (Summer 1972), 353–373.

North, Douglass C. "Capital Formation in the United States During the Early Period of Industrialization: A Reexamination of the Issues." Paper delivered at the *Second International Conference of Economic History, Aix-en Provence, 1962,* Paris, 1965.

———. "Ocean Freight Rates and Economic Development, 1750–1913." *Journal of Economic History,* 18 (December 1958), 537–555.

Parker, William N. "Agriculture." In *American Economic Growth.* Ed. Lance

E. Davis et al. New York: Harper and Row, 1972. Pp. 369–408.

———. "The Land, Minerals, Water, and Forests." In ibid. Pp. 93–119.

———. "Sources of Agricultural Productivity in the Nineteenth Century." *Journal of Farm Economics*, 49 (1967), 1455–1468.

———, and Judith L. V. Klein. "Productivity Growth in Grain Production in the United States, 1840–60 and 1900–10." In *Output, Employment, and Productivity in the United States After 1800*. Ed. Dorothy Brady. Conference on Research in Income and Wealth, National Bureau of Economic Research. Vol. 30, *Studies in Income and Wealth*. New York: Columbia University Press, 1966. Pp. 523–579.

———, and Franklee Whartenby. "The Growth of Output Before 1840." In *Trends in the American Economy During the Nineteenth Century*. Ed. William N. Parker. Conference on Research in Income and Wealth, National Bureau of Economic Research. Vol. 24, *Studies in Income and Wealth*. Princeton: Princeton University Press, 1960. Pp. 191–216.

Potter, James. "The Growth of Population in America, 1700–1860." In *Population in History: Essays in Historical Demography*. Eds. D. V. Glass and D. E. C. Eversley. Chicago: Aldine, 1965.

Poulson, Barry W. "Estimates of the Value of Manufacturing Output in the Early Nineteenth Century." *Journal of Economic History*, 29 (September 1969), 521–525.

Rosenberg, Nathan. "Technological Change." In *American Economic Growth*. Ed. Lance E. Davis et al. New York: Harper and Row, 1972. Pp. 233–279.

———. "Technological Change in the Machine Tool Industry, 1840–1910." *Journal of Economic History*, 23 (December 1963), 414–443.

Rothstein, Morton. "The Antebellum South as a Dual Economy: A Tentative Hypothesis." *Agricultural History*, 41 (October 1967), 373–382.

———. "Antebellum Wheat and Cotton Exports: A Contrast in Marketing Organization and Economic Development." *Agricultural History*, 40 (April 1966), 91–100.

Scheiber, Harry N. "Economic Change in the Civil War Era: An Analysis of Recent Studies." *Civil War History*. II (December 1965), 396–411.

Schultz, Theodore W. "Capital Formation by Education." *Journal of Political Economy*, 68 (December 1960), 571–583.

———. "Education and Economic Growth." In *Social Forces Influencing American Education*, Yearbook of the American Society for the Study of Education. Chicago, 1961. Pt. II, Ch. 3.

Smolensky, Eugene. "The Past and Present Poor." In *The Concept of Poverty*. First Report of the Task Force on Economic Growth and Opportunity. Washington, D. C.: Chamber of Commerce of the United States, 1965.

Soltow, Lee. "Economic Inequality in the United States in the Period from 1790 to 1860." *Journal of Economic History*, 31 (December 1971), 822–839.

Stigler, George J. "The Division of Labor Is Limited by the Extent of the Market." *Journal of Political Economy*, 59 (June 1951), 185–193.

Sylla, Richard. "Federal Policy, Banking Market Structure, and Capital Mobilization in the United States, 1863–1913." *Journal of Economic History*, 29 (December 1969), 657–686.

Taylor, George Rogers."American Economic Growth Before 1840: An Exploratory Essay." *Journal of Economic History*, 24 (December 1964), 427–444.

Towne, Marvin W., and Wayne D. Rasmussen. "Farm Gross Product and Gross Investment in the United States." In *Trends in the American Economy During the Nineteenth Century.* Ed. William N. Parker. Conference on Research in Income and Wealth, National Bureau of Economic Research. Vol. 24, *Studies in Income and Wealth.* Princeton: Princeton University Press, 1960. Pp. 255–312.

Uselding, Paul J. "Factor Substitution and Labor Productivity Growth in American Manufacturing, 1839–1899." *Journal of Economic History*, 32 (September 1972), 670–681.

Williamson, Jeffrey G. "Ante-Bellum Urbanization in the American Northeast." *Journal of Economic History*, 25 (October 1965), 592–608.

———, and Joseph A. Swanson. "The Growth of Cities in the American Northeast, 1820–1870." *Explorations in Enttrepreneurial History*, 4 (Supplement 1966).

Woodbury, Robert S. "The Legend of Eli Whitney and Interchangeable Parts." *Technology and Culture*, 2 (Summer 1960), 235–253.

Wright, Gavin. "Economic Democracy' and the Concentration of Agricultural Wealth in the Cotton South, 1850–1860." In *The Structure of the Cotton Economy of the Antebellum South.* Ed. William N. Parker. Washington, D.C.: Agricultural History Society, 1970. Pp. 63–93.

Zevin, Robert Brook. "The Growth of Cotton Textile Production After 1815." In *The Reinterpretation of American Economic History.* Eds. Robert W. Fogel and Stanley L. Engerman. New York: Harper and Row, 1971. Pp. 122–147.

INDEX

151